AN OHIO BUSINESSMAN'S JOURNEY:

My Journey into Darkness

Lawrence DeWitt Jones

ISBN: 0692266844
ISBN 13: 9780692266847

AUTHOR'S NOTE

T HERE COMES A TIME IN ONE'S LIFE when the truth must be told, whatever the cost. I am sure that the contents of this book will upset various groups of people, but I will not apologize for causing these reactions. Many times the perception or misperception of who we are and how we think can prevent entry into mainstream society.

I contend that the content of this book is true and factual, unless otherwise identified. If anyone should contest any of its content, the author is willing to submit to an independent polygraph test, under the condition the person contesting the content also agree to submit to an independent polygraph test.

I feel confident that my life experiences have earned me the right to share the information written in this book. I have lived in both the white man's world and the black man's world—my world. The experiences I've had in my sixty-five years of living could fill two lifetimes.

I want to thank my wife, Barbara; daughters, Tara and Galan; my son, Bennett; and my sister, Dr. Brenda Jones-Harding, for their prayers and never-dying love and financial support. I also thank my brothers, Rudolph and Otis; Reverend Dr. William S. Wheatley, his wife, Geneva, and daughter, Angela; Reverend Dr. Cheviene and Berta Jones; Reverend Franklin and Anna Carter; Delbert and Sydney Lancaster; Reverend Gary Hearst and wife Connie; Reverend Dr. Carl Small, and Bill and Dorothy Locke. I also want to thank the many members of Jones Chapel AME Church.

I also want to thank Detectives Cunningham and Finch for performing such a thorough investigation of me and my activities. Their investigation revealed evidence from the year 2000, $2,000,000 loan fraud, that was committed against, Erie Shores Computer, Barbara and I, and FirstMerit Bank. It appears the evidence uncovered, provided Cunningham and Finch an understanding of how the fraudulent activities in the Star Beverage Inc., Delaware, bank loan fraud five years prior, were related to my state and federal criminal cases.

PROLOGUE

I grew up in the 1950s and '60s on a farm owned by my parents in Durham County, North Carolina. The family's land was surrounded by landowners that were either members of the Ku Klux Klan or Klan sympathizers. I lived and worked with our Klan neighbors until I departed for college in 1967. During my time on the farm, there was only one overtly racist incident that I can remember that occurred between my family and our Klan neighbors. Over the years, the relationships between my family and our neighbors would develop and become relationships based on trust and confirmed with handshakes.

One would think that I would have horror stories to tell you about the relationship between my family and our Klan neighbors, but I don't. Some of the main horror stories that I will share with you in this book occurred after I became a successful businessman, approximately thirty years later.

The destruction of my successful technology firm, my family's small financial fortune, and my reputation was not caused by members of the Klan or other white persons. This destruction was caused by two male African American medical doctors, a male African American businessman, and a male African American attorney.

My family and I and the Klan families surrounding us developed a level of mutual trust and respect for each other. That trust and respect lead to successful business transactions between my family and our neighbors—business relationships that only required a verbal commitment and a handshake. Therefore, years later, I was sure that I could put at least that same amount of trust in four well-educated, professional African Americans.

It was impossible for me to logically comprehend what had happened to my family as Barbara and I sat there in the $500,000 home that we had owned prior to the sheriff's sale. I was attempting to make some logical sense of the horrifying seven-year journey my family and I had just endured, knowing that this dark journey would surely continue.

What happened during those seven years changed the life I had built from being recognized as one of the most well-known and successful African American businessmen and civic leaders in the state of Ohio to having lost all business and personal assets and all credibility in the eyes of the public. And now I am waiting to begin serving a thirty-seven-month sentence in a federal prison.

How did I lose the millions that Barbara and I had worked so hard to earn over the prior twenty-five years? Why did I now harbor so many negative feelings and a total lack of trust in the US Justice system and the African American population, including black businessmen and businesswomen?

CHAPTER ONE

For the first forty-nine years of my life, I believed that people were inherently good and trustworthy. I also believed that good would always overpower evil, but reality would prove me wrong during the following seven years of my life.

When the evil ones came, the forces they brought against me, my family, and my businesses destroyed everything that Barbara and I had worked to achieve during the past twenty-five years. Sixteen years later, I am no closer to understanding how these evil ones were able to take over and control my decision making and actions.

I continue to believe, as I have for most of my life, that there is a God Spirit that controls the universes. I also believed that same supernatural force would always protect me from the evil forces.

In December of 1999, my family and I were celebrating at Disney in Orlando, Florida, awaiting the end of the millennium and oblivious to what the future had in store for us—a future that would lead me to question whether evil powers were more powerful than good powers in our society.

While growing up, my parents attended church every Sunday and insisted that my siblings and I attend with them. This demand continued until we were in a position to make our own decision regarding our church attendance.

Religion was important to me during that period of my life. As I aged and experienced more, logic began to interfere more and more with my immature religious beliefs. By the time I was in college—a college supported by a protestant church—I had many unanswered questions about religion and those who were teaching and living a "religious" life. After my first year at Johnson C. Smith University, I abandoned religion, but even at that time, I knew in my mind and heart that there had to be some all-knowing spirit—a God Spirit that controlled the universes. My logic told me that the Big Bang Theory was true, and that this God Spirit caused or permitted this action to take place. Logic told me that the lifespan of men and women was much too short to even begin to discover and understand the unknowns of creation and this God Spirit. Even when we compile and add to what we know, generation after generation, we continue to be eons away from this understanding. Because of my thought process and the little that I understand and my inner being, I have evolved from being a religious person to beginning the process of becoming a spiritual person.

During those seven years of existing and living in the depths of hell (late 1999–2006), it was like I was looking through a one-way window and seeing things happen to me and against me, and I had no control over the outcome. The more logical decisions I made, the more damaging the results.

I had been a successful businessman for fifteen years. Logistics, problem solving, and decision making had been the strongest of my strong points, but during those seven years, my strengths became my weaknesses. During this seven-year time frame, I made seven major decisions—decisions that I felt confident would, if not prevent my firms from financial disaster, at least stop the financial losses. But each of the seven logical decisions I made would only thrust my family and businesses deeper into the abyss.

Only after waking one night from an extremely vivid nightmare did it become clear to me that my problems had not been caused by my decision making. As my visions and thought processes became clearer, the level of anxiety and fear became almost unbearable. I was sweating; my skin was now clammy; and my heart was about to burst out of my chest.

As clear as one can see daylight, I could now understand who was causing my problems. I had permitted five sociopaths to weave themselves into my firm and into the core decision making of my business operations. What was unfortunate and tragic for me was that it was too late to stop the devastation.

The actions of these sociopathic individuals would prove to be devastating to my family life and would totally destroy the business that Barbara and I had toiled and sacrificed for years to build.

Everyone who has dealt with a sociopath—whether in your family, with a friend, or as a business associate or partner—will understand immediately the dangerous journey on which I am about to take you. As you journey with me, those of you who have not experienced having a sociopath in your life will clearly understand the dangers and devastation these individuals can bring into your lives. One sociopath in your life can cause devastation; try to imagine the total devastation that five sociopaths can cause. (See the definition of *sociopath* below.)

My story may read like fiction, but I can assure you, what you are about to read is true and accurate.

Sociopath: A persons with a psychopathic personality whose behavior is antisocial, often criminal, and who lacks a sense of moral responsibility or social conscience. These persons have no sense of right or wrong and are incapable of caring or loving and believe that everything they do is right.

CHAPTER TWO

My African American (Negro) parents never had to tell their children that they could grow up to be whatever they wanted to be, or that they were equal to anyone, or that respect and honor were important because they lived each day displaying all of these qualities to my sister, six brothers, and me. The eight of us grew up with great respect for our parents. We addressed our parents as "Mama" and "Daddy" and answered them with a "yes, ma'am" and "yes, sir." We did this until my father died in 1982, and Mama passed away in 2006.

My parents, Willie Lee and Elsie Smith Jones, were from different sides of the Negro tracks.

Daddy stood six feet two inches tall, very handsome, with a body fat of less than six percent. My father's complexion stated clearly that no white master had interfered in his gene line.

My mother was a very beautiful lady. There was clear evidence that the white master had been very active in my mother's gene line; her completion confirmed that fact.

The true history of slavery will include the fact that when Africans were captured to be transported to the colonies, many of the strong-willed Africans escaped capture or were killed attempting to escape. Of those strong Africans who were captured, many died or were killed during the long voyage to the colonies. Of those strong Africans that survived the trip to the colonies, some were killed attempting to escape, and others were used as a sacrifice to dissuade others from escape attempts.

After almost all of the strong-willed slaves had been eliminated, the slave masters now had only to deal with the male and female slaves who were too frightened to rebel in any way. Only a small number of those strong, defiant, and rebellious African slaves remained to carry the fight forward. It appears that my father and mother were from a line of the defiant and rebellious African slaves.

⊷⊶

Mr. Melvin Parish was the leader of the local Klan chapter. He and his family lived less than a mile down the dirt road from our house. Shaw Road was an unpaved country road, approximately ten miles from the city of Durham, North Carolina.

My parents had achieved a feat that very few blacks (Negros) had achieved in the south in the 1940: they had purchased 396 acres of land. These 396 acres were bordered on all sides by Ku Klux Klan members or Klan sympathizers.

The Klan and their sympathizers had a very visible ritual that they performed every fourth Saturday night. In a large field, approximately halfway between our property and the property owned by Mr. Vester Keith, the father of my future wife, the Klan would burn a fifty-foot-high cross. That burning cross would light up the sky for miles.

Mr. Parish and his twin boys were always present at the cross burning, and whenever my older brothers would see them during the week, they would let them know they had seen them burning their cross on Saturday night. Daddy and Mama warned us of the dangers of many in the white race, especially those who were members of the Klan. There were only a few black families that did not have great fear of the Klan, and my family was one of those families.

My brother Rudolph shared the following story with me, and my mother confirmed it numerous times prior to her passing: My parents kept a small herd of cows in the pasture where our livestock barn stood. Mr. Parish owned a large black stud bull. Area farmers would rent Mr. Parish's bull and pay hundreds of dollars for breeding purposes. Mr. Parish had a habit of permitting his stud bull to roam the neighborhood freely. My father was concerned about the big monster of an animal harming the small children in the neighborhood; therefore, he suggested to Mr. Parish that he should keep his bull contained. A week or so after my daddy's request, Mr. Parish's bull returned to our property. During the next few weeks, my father repeated his request to Mr. Parish a second and third time, with no success. The next time the bull showed up, my father warned Mr. Parish that if his bull came on his property again, he would shoot that bull. I am sure that Mr. Parish, the leader of the KKK, never in his wildest dreams thought that Willie Lee Jones, a black man, would shoot his prized stud bull; therefore, he did not take my father's warning seriously.

It was only a few days later when this massive black animal made his next visit to my daddy's land. What our father did next shocked everyone in the family. He got his double-barrel shotgun from the rack in the closet, loaded it with buckshot shells, and strolled outside to confront the bull. As he approached this massive animal, the bull turned toward my father but immediately turned again and began to run. This was when the shot rang out from my daddy's gun. This large fearless animal had been shot in the ass with buckshot.

Daddy knew that the buckshot would not be fatal but would draw blood, including blood from his massive and very valuable scrotum sac and testicles.

This was probably the only time that everyone in the family, including my mother, felt real fear of a possible violent confrontation with the Parish family and the Klan. The speed of the bull's exit confirmed his pain, and that he would arrive home within a short period of time. The family also knew that once Mr. Parish saw the animal in its condition, he would know that my daddy had fulfilled his promise.

It was less than two hours later when Mr. Parrish come racing down the dry dirt road toward our home. The cloud of dust that followed after his vehicle came to a stop and temporarily covered him and his truck. A few seconds later, Mr. Parish was visible again.

Mama told Daddy not to go into the yard to meet Mr. Parish, but the family knew that once Daddy's mind was made up, there was no changing it. Mr. Parish remained in his truck, parked in the road. Daddy told everyone to stay in the house and ignored Mama as she begged him not to go outside. My father not only entered the yard; he proceeded to approach Mr. Parish's vehicle. As soon as Mr. Parish saw Daddy approaching, he yelled out, "Willie, damn it', you shot my goddamn bull!"

Mr. Parish, I am sure, could not believe it when my father entered the road and arrived at his vehicle and then proceeded to extend his head inside the passenger's window and state to him: "Mr. Parish, I told you that I would shoot your bull if it came on my property again, and I shot him." Being a man of God, Daddy seldom cursed.

No one will ever know what was going through Mr. Parish's mind as my father approached his vehicle. Was it fear, surprise, anger, or all of all of the above? We will never know because after my father finished what he had to say, he turned his back on Mr. Parish and returned to the yard and into the house. I think I can truthfully say that no African American (Negro) had ever taken action against or spoken to Mr. Parish (the leader of the KKK) as my father had done. I would even venture to say that no white man had treated Mr. Parish or his property as my father had done. I can assure you that everyone in our house felt some fear after Daddy's actions that day.

In what seemed an eternity but was probably only a few seconds, Mr. Parish, without any additional comments, performed a quick U-turn in that dirt road and disappeared into the dust.

Of course, the family had some ongoing concerns about possible repercussions against the family related to Daddy's historic confrontation that day on that dirt road.

A few years later, my father's brother was helping Mr. Parish's people cut timber, and a tree "accidentally" fell on Uncle Earle and killed him. The official ruling of his death was "an accident," due to the men drinking alcohol. Not a lot of investigating was done to get specific details of the accident. All of the witnesses gave the same story: "the death of Uncle Earle was an accident because everyone had been drinking while cutting timber that day."

CHAPTER THREE

The Klan was real, and our family members were neighbors to many of them. As relationships formed and as the years passed, a high level of mutual respect evolved between my family and theirs. We didn't visit each other's homes or socialize together, but mutual respect was the norm.

I will always have doubts about the "accident" that killed my uncle that day in those woods. My father took the news of his brother's death hard, but he and the family moved on with living and assisting Uncle Earle's widow and children.

Years later when Mr. Parish died, my parents and older brothers visited the wake and took food to show their condolences. When my father passed in 1982, Parish's widow and sons attended the wake and brought food. In 2006, my mother passed, and the Parish sons come to the wake and brought food.

This show of condolences and respect was displayed through the years as many of the other neighbors needed help or when someone passed away.

CHAPTER FOUR

T alk about hard work! Growing up on a tobacco farm required working six days a week. From a very early age I worked on my parents' farm. We grew up quite healthy. The hard work included raising cows, hogs, and chickens; planting large vegetable gardens; cropping corn, tobacco, and wheat; and cutting and hauling pine wood for pulp production.

The abundance from working the farm and selling pine trees for pulp production put the family in a position of being self-sufficient and made ours one of the top income-producing families in the greater community. Tobacco harvesting and selling wood for pulp were the two major income producers for the family.

The government controlled how much tobacco acreage we could plant, thus controlling the amount of profit in tobacco we could make annually. The pulp wood business was much harder than farming but much more profitable. In an average year, the family would make two to three time the profit from pulp wood than profits from tobacco harvesting. It was not unusual for us to work six days a week during the summer and fall months.

When we did have a free day, we would sometimes help the neighbors with their tobacco harvesting. My father would never require us to assist the neighbors; he always permitted us to decide if we wanted to work additional hours.

The type of farming we did and the extreme weight lifting involved in wood for pulp production were very hard and tiresome, but our energy and dedication came as a result of knowing that this hard work was for our family and not for someone else. Almost all of the other black (Negro) families did not own their land; therefore, they lived and worked on land owned by white people. The parents of my future wife owned their land. Most families were sharecroppers, meaning that they farmed the land owned by whites, and most of the time, they borrowed money from the landowners because they had no bank accounts; therefore, they had no access to bank loans. This practice all but assured the sharecropper family very little or no profit annually and revolving indebtedness to the land owner.

CHAPTER FIVE

Living in the County of Durham, North Carolina, ten miles from the nearest town, surely kept my siblings and me from major mischief and trouble. The nearest school for blacks (Negros) was approximately nine miles from our farm. To arrive at our segregated school, we would travel past two white schools.

I never had a second thought about attending the white schools because we had an excellent school to attend. Merrick Moore, the school I attended, educated students from the first grade through the twelfth grade. I didn't realize it at the time, but I would later appreciate the excellent, dedicated teachers and administrators who provided Merrick Moore students exceptional educational opportunities.

These teachers and staff provided an atmosphere of learning and caring. They treated us as their extended family. I graduated from Merrick Moore in 1967, two years prior to court-ordered school integration in

North Carolina. My younger brother and sister can better provide the contrast between attending the segregated Merrick Moore and then, after integration, attending the former all-white Southern High School.

I think it appropriate that I share this special story with you. My sister, Brenda, was the youngest and smartest of all of the siblings. I know my parents were elated to have a girl after seven boys. Brenda spent her junior and senior years at Southern High School. She and her counselor at Merrick Moore kept in touch after her transfer to Southern High School. Continuing this contact would prove to be a critical decision for Brenda. The Southern High counselor had a meeting with Brenda and suggested that she focus on attending a trade school. Brenda had become a mentally strong person and knew that this counselor had provided guidance about Brenda's future, based her racist perspective. Brenda was astute enough to contact her former counselor, and she began helping Brenda on a regular basis. With this guidance and assistance, Brenda continued to excel in her grades, and her SAT score propelled her to a position where a number of Ivy League Universities began to show real interest.

After numerous offers, Brenda decided to accept a full scholarship to Brown University, where she graduate in three and a half years, with a premed degree. She then attended the University of North Carolina at Chapel Hill where she received her doctor of medicine degree. After that, Brenda enrolled at the University of Tennessee at Memphis and received her doctor of ophthalmology degree.

My sister then enlisted in the US Navy as a commissioned officer, and after four years of distinguished service to her country, Brenda began her successful medical career as a civilian.

My younger brother Otis played football at Southern, and his talents earned him a football scholarship to play with me at Johnson C. Smith. I was pleased to have him join me and play linebacker on the strong side, where I played defensive end.

CHAPTER SIX

Farming and hauling pulpwood were great income producers for the family but this was hard manual labor, and I was looking for a way out.

All of my brothers and I were above average in height, size, and strength; therefore, it was natural for us to play sports. I was fortunate to attend Merrick Moore at the time when there were both basketball and football teams. I excelled at both sports, never having to lift any official weights because the pulpwood had been the source for my weight-lifting requirements.

I had the pleasure of playing football with two of my brothers while at Merrick Moore. I have fun memories of playing the offensive tackle position and Alex (Gino) playing the guard position beside me. We were so good that we would alert the defensive tackle and guard positioned in front of us where our running back would carry the ball because we were confident that they would not have the ability to stop the play. I served as captain of the football team and basketball team my sophomore, junior, and senior years.

I excelled in basketball and football and received all-state honors in both sports. After receiving offers from Johnson C. Smith University (JCSU), Duke University, North Carolina Central University, Michigan State, and A & T University, I decided to attend JCSU.

Duke University was in my hometown, and in the 1960s, it was well known that many African American athletes were guided into classes such as basket weaving because it was assumed that black athletes could not succeed academically in regular classes.

After a heart-to-heart talk with Eddie McGirt, the Johnson C. Smith University (JCSU) football coach, I was convinced that attending JCSU was the right decision to make. I knew that if I worked hard in my classes, I would graduate with a degree of importance. I now had to find a way to inform the manager of the Durham Sporting Goods Company, who was my Duke mentor and promoter, that I had decided to attend Johnson C. Smith instead of Duke.

I enrolled at JCSU in the fall of 1967. My brother Gino had decided to join the army the year prior.

My freshman year at JCSU was a year of great football, but it was also a year of homesickness, due to being away from my girlfriend, whom I had known since I was three, and she two, years old. I must admit: I did very little studying, but I passed all of my freshman courses but one—French.

After my freshman year, in order to play football in my sophomore year, I would be required to remove the failing grade in French. I had also been listed by the US Army with a draft rating of A-1, meaning that I was available and had no obstacles to prevent me from being drafted into the US Army.

It was the meeting I had with my JCSU counselor that summer that shocked me into understanding the importance of studying and receiving passing grades. My counselor was a retired US Marine. You must remember that the Vietnam War had been active for a number of years, and this was the summer of 1968, the year of the Tat Offensive in the Vietnam War. My counselor, after a few minutes into our session, suggested that I would have a better future if I joined the military.

After that meeting with my counselor, I knew that the U S military was not a good option at the time. My brother Willie had completed a tour in Nam and had escaped with his life because he had been wounded and was recuperating in Japan when his entire squad was ambushed. My brother Gino, a second lieutenant, also served a year in Nam. He had left me his Pontiac GTO to drive while he was gone.

Both brothers advised me to avoid a tour in Vietnam if at all possible. I successfully enrolled in summer school, knowing my second choice was unacceptable. I had no funds to cover the cost of my summer classes, my food, or a place to stay, but I was now committed to succeed as never before.

My success came that summer because I was able to locate a room in the freshman dorm with a broken lock. This is where I stayed during the summer session. I was also able to get a job at the UPS facility in Charlotte, working the third shift. My meals were made up of mostly banana sandwiches, water, and pop that summer.

After that summer, I had learned my lesson, and I applied myself academically the duration of my three years at JCSU.

CHAPTER SEVEN

I was just an eighteen-year-old country boy when I made my decision to attend Johnson C. Smith University. I had never spent more than a week at a time away from the wide-open spaces and security of home.

I made all-state in football and basketball, but I remained skeptical about my ability to make the Golden Bulls football squad. That skepticism only lasted for a few days into summer scrimmages. After my play abilities were observed, I was ahead of two seniors who played the defensive end and linebacker positions; my confidence was gaining momentum. I not only had become aware that I could make the team, but I also knew that, in time, I could probably play my way to a position on the first-team defense.

Well, history will show that my athletic and football skills won me a starting position at defensive end, and my leadership skills put me in a position to become captain of the defense and co-captain of the team in my sophomore year. I knew that I had one obstacle ahead of me if I was to maintain those leadership positions. That obstacle was a junior defensive tackle named Edgar Farmer. Edger stood about six feet two inches tall and weighed in at two hundred seventy-five pounds. The team called him "Big Red." Big Red was sure that I wanted his job as captain of the defense.

It was a hot day in August 1967 when Coach Charlie Cox decided to punish the defense for not following instructions and ordered the defense over to "the chute."

The chute was simply a five-foot long by approximately three-foot wide space, fenced in by iron poles, with each end open. Normally, it involved a defensive player lining up at one end and an offensive player at the other, and when the whistle blew, there would be a collision somewhere in the middle of "the chute." The winner of the duel would exit from the opposition's end of "the chute."

On this special day it would be defense against defense. After about twenty minutes of elimination, it was down to Big Red and me. I weighed in at around 195 pounds and Big Red at 275. That day Big Red and the entire defense became aware of the fact that there was a new leader in town. Edger would test my physical strength again later in the month while on the sidelines, during a practice session. Big Red could hardly believe it when I broke away from his grasp and picked him up and slammed him to the ground. After that, Edger and I became good friends and powerful teammates. At the beginning of Edger's senior year, he was rated the third best defensive tackle in the nation.

In 1969, the Johnson C. Smith University Golden Bulls won the CIAA Football Championship. No JCSU team before or after equaled our 1969 championship feat. I would play at JCSU for four years and earn All-American status my junior and senior years.

My first college football game was against Tuskegee University; Lionel Richie and the Commodores were students at Tuskegee at the time and would soon be discovered.

In August of 1967, we traveled to Tuskegee, Alabama, to play Tuskegee University's football team. The stadium was little more than a pasture, with only a few seats on the visitors' side. The teams were pretty evenly matched in talent; therefore, the score was close throughout the game. It was midway through the fourth quarter when a fight erupted while our offense was on the field.

I remember both benches clearing onto the field. I ran onto the field, looking for someone to confront. Approximately twenty yards in front of me I saw my enemy holding a bucket in one hand. The sun was extremely bright, and the bucket was reflecting the sun's glare— a daytime game in Alabama in September.

I decided that this was the enemy I would defeat and defeat quickly. As I started toward him, he began approaching me. When we reached the distance of approximately ten yards apart, the enemy reached into this bucket he was carrying and pulled out what appeared to be a long butcher's knife.

In my shock, amazement, and fear, my feet automatically did a U-turn, and I was headed back to my sidelines in a sprint. I am not sure how long the enemy pursued me, but I returned safely to my side of the field. The fight was stopped, and we went on the win the game.

It was my freshman year, and we were undefeated going into Atlanta, Georgia, to play Morris Brown University. Coach had reserved rooms for the team in the Pascals Hotel, in downtown Atlanta. As co-captain, I should have known that this would be an interesting trip to Atlanta, the mecca of the south. I, along with members of the team, entered the elevator for the third floor, and just before the doors closed, a beautiful lady entered the elevator holding a poodle. She got off on the second floor, and knowing that she had all of our un-divided attention, once she exited and prior to the doors closing for the ride to the third floor, this lady bent over to put her poodle on the floor, and the short, short skirt revealed that she was not wearing panties. You can imagine the level of excitement in that elevator on our way to the third floor.

Later that evening, around 10:00 p.m., a good thirty minutes after we were supposed to have been in our rooms for the evening, we were instead partying in the rooms of two young ladies, per their invita-tion. The room was so crowded that no one saw Coach McGirt and Coach Cox enter the room. The party ended, and everyone returned to their rooms knowing that we would pay dearly for this brief eve-ning of fun and enjoyment.

We won the game that next day with three seconds remaining in the fourth quarter. Coach McGirt, "Cutt," as we called him, had checked us out of the hotel prior to the game; therefore, we traveled from Atlanta, Georgia, to Charlotte, North Carolina, in our uniforms. The grueling practice session that following Monday afternoon left most of us too sick and tired to even eat dinner.

My junior year when we traveled to Atlanta to play Morris Brown, we stayed in a hotel approximately twenty-five miles outside of Atlanta. Coach McGirt made sure that we did not repeat the Pascal 1967 incident.

⊷⊷ ⊶⊶

Our parents (Barbara Keith's and mine) were two of the African American families that were landowners in Durham County. They said that Barbara and I played together and liked each other when I was three and she was two years old. Between the third grade and sixth grade, she became my girlfriend. She was one of the pretties and smartest girls at Merrick Moore. Before leaving for Johnson C. Smith my freshman year, I told Barbara not to worry about me meeting someone else because no one could ever take her place. I held out during my freshman year, but during my sophomore year, not able to resist any longer, I came home for Easter break, and Barbara and I were married on April 5, 1969. Our first beautiful child, Tara, was born on October 26, 1969. It was great that I was able to be with Barbara when Tara was born. JCSU had traveled to Raleigh to play Shaw University. After the game, I was allowed to go home to Durham instead of returning with the team to Charlotte. Tara was born while I was home that weekend.

Barbara did not visit campus often, but I was able to talk her and my sister, Brenda, into bringing Tara to JCSU for a Saturday visit so the guys could meet my beautiful wife and daughter. Barbara and Brenda still, to this day, comment that we totally ignored them and my friends, and I focused our total attention on Tara.

Carter Hall is where I stayed my freshman year—an old, poorly kept building with small rooms that housed two students in each room. There were two restrooms on each floor, which accommodated approximately fifty students. Many times while attending JCSU, I would remember those beautiful, spacious rooms that I had seen while visiting Duke University, prior to committing to attend JCSU.

My brother Alexander (Gino) chose to enlist in the army prior to continuing his higher education. Prior to leaving for his tour in Vietnam, he loaned me his GTO to have on campus during my freshman year at JCSU. Beginning in my sophomore year, I had to rely on an old 1957 beetle to make the 150-mile trip from Durham to Charlotte. That old beetle was a lifesaver, but after many, many round trips to and from Durham over a two-year period, it began to run on only three cylinders. This made the 150-mile trip on I-85 quite long. To shorten the trip I learned to catch the wind draft of the tractor-trailer rigs, and that wind draft would increase my speed between six and ten miles per hour.

During my senior year, I decided to allow many of my teammates to use the beetle. Those who had permission to use it knew where the ignition key was kept. After a while, my beetle was given the name "the football team's car."

After driving my unbreakable VW home to Durham for the last time after graduation, I realized that Barbara did not have transportation, so prior to departing for the Dallas Cowboys training camp, I installed a rebuilt engine in the beetle for her to drive.

CHAPTER EIGHT

During my freshman year, many of the freshman students, both men and women, did not make it past the first semester. They found the student union building, and they proceeded to make it their home. They hung out there, played cards and other games there, listened to music there, and forgot to go to class.

JCSU had many beautiful ladies in attendance, and one of those young ladies was crowned Miss JCSU. She was extremely beautiful, smart, friendly, and humble. She made friends with many students, male and female. Unfortunately at the time, she became close friends with one of her lesbian classmates. Because of this relationship, she was outed on campus and was stripped of her title as Miss JCSU. That's how life was in the late 1960 at a protestant African American university.

Johnson C. Smith is located approximately two miles from downtown Charlotte, North Carolina. Of course, being a predominately black university, the campus was located in an area of the city where the majority of the population were African American.

One of the regional banks operated a branch across Batiesford Road, the main street that connected the campus to the rest of the city. I would have checks cashed periodically at this bank. On one occasion while cashing a check, the teller, a young African American male, cashed my check and proceeded to offer me a nickel bag of marijuana from his teller window.

My roommate during my sophomore year was Steve Brown, a young man from the Southside of Chicago. Steve was very street-wise, and after a time, we became friends. One Saturday evening after the JCSU Golden Bulls had demolished an opponent, Steve and I were planning how we would spend the evening. Although we did not hang out together often, Steve had been attempting to get me to smoke a joint. I had declined his offer at least ten to fifteen times, but this evening would be different. Upon returning to the room after taking my shower, I noticed the joint and a lighter lying at the foot of my bed.

I lit the joint and took, at most, three inhales; yes, I did inhale! I had bragged to Steve that smoking marijuana would not affect me. Well, I was totally wrong. No more than sixty seconds after that last inhale, I was experienced a relaxing and mellowing feeling. After my arthritis became a problem, at times I used marijuana to relieve the pain.

JCSU was located mostly in a residential neighborhood. There were many professional, upward-bound African Americans living among the blue-collar workers.

JCSU was located on a popular section of the street, and this was where numerous groups of young blacks, who were not attending JCSU, hung out. They were given the name "block boys." Most of the block boys had dropped out of high school and were unemployed.

These young men would gather on the street corners and harass the students, especially the women, on a regular basis.

Of course, these young men and the college students they encountered would have problems relating to each other. Some of these encounters resulted in psychological confrontations and sometimes in physical abuse.

After my freshman year, because I had not applied myself in a couple of classes, I had no choice but to attend summer school in order to be eligible to play football my sophomore year. That summer was when I had my first negative encounter with the block boys. Prior to this time, I had experienced no problems because I would always speak to them, and at times I stopped and talked briefly. I became known to many of these young men as a friendly but strong, no-nonsense person who respected them.

As I mentioned prior, my brother Alex had left me his GTO while he was serving in Vietnam. One afternoon, as I drove down Tryon Street toward downtown Charlotte, I saw one of the block boys, Skeno, walking toward downtown I stopped and gave Skeno a ride to where he was going. The GTO had bucket seats, and I would, at times, carry my friend's 38 pistol between the seats. Well, that day I gave Skeno a ride, and the pistol was between the seats, and Skeno commented, "Hey, man, are you always packing?"

I responded, "Most of the time." Skeno and I had always shown respect for each other, and after I gave him a ride that day, that level of respect grew.

There were only a few other students who knew how to keep peace with the block boys, and after many female and male students complained about how the block boys were treating them while walking down the street, we decided to advise the students, at least those who would listen. We shared with them the best and safest way to communicate with the young men who were hanging out on the corners.

Our advice was quite simple:

1. These young people are envious of us because we are in college.
2. They feel that they don't have a lot to lose if they get into trouble.
3. They are looking for some attention.
4. Therefore, when they speak to you, you should respond in a positive way and continue walking at your normal pace. Just a hello from you in response to their comments is very important to their egos.

Our advice worked most of the time for many of the students but not all of the time—not even for me.

One night prior to driving out to my third-shift job at UPS, I strolled down to the Busy Bee and bought some pork and beans and a pop to have for my meal at break time. On my way back to my dorm room, four block boys stopped me and asked what I had in the bag. I told them what was in the bag, and one of them proceeded to jerk the bag from me. I commented that the bag contained my dinner. After seeing that I was not going to have the bag returned to me, I began walking back to my dorm. After a short period of walking, I heard footsteps approaching, and a familiar voice rang out: "Hey, Jones—Skeno." I stopped and waited for Skeno to approach. When he was close enough, he handed me my bag and proceeded to apologize for the guys who had taken it. Of course, I accepted the apology and thanked him.

Not all encounters were as successful as my encounter. One male student was shot in the mouth during an encounter, and numerous females students were detained and grouped by the block boys during my four years at JCSU. Many of these block boys ended up in the Charlotte city jail or in Raleigh in the state facility.

I made two special trips to the military base in Columbia, South Carolina, during my freshman year. Not every student enters college with his or her tuition totally paid. Having a car on campus as a freshman—a sporty, beautiful one at that—made me stand out from most other athletes and was quite special. I was really appreciative and honored that Gino would leave his GTO with me.

The most memorable occasion that involved the GTO was when I was approached, in confidence, about providing three female students a ride to Columbia, South Carolina. For this trip, I would be paid one hundred dollars, and my hotel cost would be covered if an overnight stay was necessary. After becoming aware of the reason for their trip to Columbia, I accepted their offer.

I drove these three young ladies to a hotel not far from the large military base. I would learn that there were women who traveled to Columbia from all over, on the first of each month. For many years I wondered why these three ladies felt that they could trust me with their secrets. I kept their secret because I understood that they were working to pay their JCSU tuition.

I never judged or spoke about these young ladies to anyone, and I refused to judge them; after all, I was able to attend college because I used my body to play football; therefore, how could I "cast any stones?"

CHAPTER NINE

During football season, the football team would always be the last group to eat dinner before the cafeteria closed. On this particular day, I would enter the cafeteria and get in line to be served, but the line was too long, Therefore, a group of players did as we had done many times before when students had waited too long to enter the cafeteria: we proceeded to get in line in front of them.

I happened to be the last football player in line after we got in front of the other students. This put me immediately in front of the person where we all had positioned ourselves. At first I didn't notice the male student standing behind me, but a couple of minutes later, this student let me know that he did not appreciate us cutting line in front of him. I ignored him at first but decided to turn and address him. When I looked down at his hand, I glimpsed what appeared to be a knife. I asked him what he had in his hand, and he showed me the knife. For some reason, his holding that knife did not alarm or frightened me. I asked him what was he doing with a knife and ordered him to put that knife away. With fear in his eyes, he quickly put the knife away. I then turned again and involved myself in ongoing conversations with the athletes in front of me.

This knife incident happened approximately two weeks prior to the JCSU homecoming weekend. We had won the homecoming game in convincing fashion earlier that Saturday afternoon. My roommate, Herb Boyd and friend and co-captain, Elroy Duncan, and I were trying to decide if we were going to the homecoming dance when we received the news that a student from Johnson C. Smith had committed suicide by walking in front of a freight train earlier that evening.

The next morning at breakfast, we would all learn that the student who had committed suicide the evening before was the student we had cut line on and who had stood behind me in the cafeteria line that day, with the knife in his hand.

I knew that I was an extremely fortunate guy because I had escaped the dangers that I had put myself in by the actions I taken that day against a mentally unstable student.

⸺✠⸺

It was on the evening of April 4, 1968, when my world changed forever. I was in my dorm room when the news reached the students at Johnson C. Smith University that my leader, our leader, Dr. Martin Luther King Jr., had been killed. The news media did not call it an assassination; they called it a killing.

The Mayor of Charlotte and other powers that be decided quickly that Johnson C. Smith had to be closed down immediately because they felt that the students would lead the African American communities to riot.

It will never be known if the powers that be were correct because President Newsome ordered the university shut down and gave the students a deadline to be off campus. I immediately drove home to Durham, North Carolina. It took several weeks for me to realize that life had to continue without our leader. I was sure that someone else would step up and assume the mantle of Dr. King, but no one ever did take Dr. King's place. Decades had to pass before I realized that it would have been impossible for anyone to have taken Dr. King's place.

The Decade of the 1960s Was Like No Other Decade:

1. The decade of the "flower children"; Woodstock; LSD, and marijuana
2. The Civil Rights struggles
3. The Vietnam War
4. The assassination of Malcolm X
5. The assassination of President John F. Kennedy
6. The assassination of Bobby Kennedy
7. The assassination of Dr. Martin Luther King Jr.
8. The race riots

Just imagine, spending your high school and college life experiencing all of this in one decade—the decade of the sixties. There has never been a decade like the decade of the 1960s in the history of this nation.

CHAPTER TEN

I had excelled in football, earning All-American honors in my junior and senior years. Now came the time to see if one or more of the NFL teams had any interest in drafting me.

The NFL draft came and went, and no team drafted me or made contact. I was truly disappointed but knew that I had to deal with this disappointment in a mature way. My teammates were all shocked that I was not selected in the draft. Not being drafted was a total disappointment because Tim Beamer and Bernard Parker, two of my teammates, were drafted. Beamer was drafted by the Buffalo Bills and played a couple of years behind O. J. Simpson.

A day or so after the draft, I received a call from a representative of the Washington Redskins football team. Later that day, the Dallas Cowboys representative made contact. Each offered me a free-agent contract with his team. I knew that I wanted to play pro ball, but I also knew that making a team as a free agent was next to impossible without a lot of luck.

I had a decision to make: should I sign with the Washington Redskins or the Dallas Cowboys. I was really upset at both organizations because they had not thought enough of my talents to draft me.

The representative from the Washington Redskins convinced me that Washington would be the best team for my services. The representative had a plane ticket waiting for me at the Raleigh-Durham Airport. All I had to do was retrieve the ticket and board the flight for Washington, and the representative would be waiting for me at the arriving gate of Washington National Airport.

One must remember that I was a twenty-one-year-old country boy with no one in a position to assist in my decision making. I drove to the Raleigh-Durham Airport that morning with every intention of flying to Washington, DC, where I would sign as a free agent with the Washington Redskins.

I can't explain to this day how and what happened upon my arrival at the Raleigh Raleigh-Durham Airport that sunny morning. As I was proceeding to my gate to board my flight, a person called out my name and approached me and introduced himself as the Dallas Cowboys representative who had been communicating with me. How did he know that I was boarding a flight to Washington, DC, where I would sign a contract with the Redskins?

He never shared with me how he knew my itinerary for that day. He asked if he could spend a couple of minutes with me to discuss and explain the mistake I would be making if I signed with the Redskins.

Now I was even more confused; I couldn't sign with both teams. This guy told me not to catch that flight to Washington but to meet with him in his hotel room for the next hour, and after he made his presentation, if I wanted to proceed to Washington, he would fly me there in the Cowboys' private jet.

I agreed to accompany him to his room. The meeting lasted for approximately an hour, and at the end of this meeting, this guy had convinced me to sign a free-agent agreement with his Dallas Cowboys—right there in his hotel room.

This free-agent agreement carried a $1,500 signing bonus and at least a dozen "if clauses." If I was successful in fulfilling those "if clauses," my annual salary would increase from $15,000 to approximately $60,000. What I wasn't aware of was that most of those "if clauses" were next to impossible to fulfill.

I never made that flight to Washington, and the next day I received a call from a highly pissed-off Redskin representative. When I informed him that I had decided to sign as a free agent with the Dallas Cowboys, he stated, "Jones we have nothing else to discuss," and he hung up. I knew that I had betrayed the Redskins' representative, but I had made my decision—good or bad, right or wrong.

The first order of business after signing was to travel to Dallas, Texas for a two day introduction session with the Dallas Cowboys administrative staff. How well I remember being on the bus with approximately twenty other rookies as we travelled from the Dallas airport to the Sheraton Hotel in downtown Dallas. As the bus pulled up to the hotel where we would exit, there was a group of beautiful ladies surrounding the bus. As we exited the bus we were engulfed by these women. Most just wanted to touch us and say hi. Others handed out cards containing their names and phone numbers. On the second evening after completing our session, a few of us walked down the street to a sports lounge. When we announced to the manager that we were draftees of the Cowboys, we could not pay for anything ordered that entire evening. We were treated like royalty.

Over the years, whenever I would read about the hundreds of pro athletes who were trapped or caught-up by these young women, I understood how this could happen. This is easy to understand when one remembers that these young men ranged in ages from twenty to twenty two years, Most had never experienced anything close to what they were now experiencing. It was like a Hollywood atmosphere for these young men. The adult decision-making wisdom would not become a part of these young men until years later; for many of them years too late.

Summer camp for the Cowboys was held in Thousand Oaks, California, at the beautiful and wealthy California Lutheran University, nestled in an upper-class community. This trip was my first time to California and the West Coast. I arrived at the Los Angeles Airport, where Cowboy representatives met me and drove me to the CLU campus.

After arriving at camp, it was probably three hours before any one of the thirty-plus players who had arrived even spoke to me. I would later realize why only a few of the guys present were in a talkative mood. Those were the low draft choices. The high draft choices and free agents were subdued and silent, as though in a foreign land. We were directed to our campus rooms. These dorm rooms made the rooms at JCSU look like closets.

My first roommate was Ron J. Ron, who would go on and excel in the NFL, receiving All-Pro honors with the Los Angeles Rams for a number of years.

The camp atmosphere was cold and intimidating. No friendships were formed during those first three weeks of practice. I had made

Small College All- American twice, but now I was competing against pro athletes and the new guys who were either small college or major university All-Americans.

My first challenge was passing the physical examination. I had stretched ligaments in both knees with enough damage that the condition had provided me a military medical deferment in the summer of 1968.

I will always remember that when it was time for the Cowboys' elderly doctor to check my knees, he was distracted by one of his assistants. When he continued with my exam, he omitted my knee examination totally. I knew that I had been very fortunate because I was pretty sure that a thorough exam of my knees would have caused the failure of my physical examination.

Coach Tubbs was the Dallas linebacker coach. All draftees and free agents looking to play linebacker reported to Coach Tubbs the morning after arrival. I was well aware that Dallas already had a number of All-Pro linebackers and a strong stable of second-string linebackers also. Now I was looking at thirty guys who were fighting for, at most, one or two possible spots on the team at the linebacker position.

One must remember that this was 1971, only a few years after schools had been desegregated in the south. Of the approximate thirty athletes interested in winning a linebacker position, ten were white. The elimination process was quite interesting. The black and white linebackers were separated during the first week of practice sessions. This meant the white athletics eliminated each other, and the black athletes eliminated each other. This separate process appeared to be done to assure the team that it would have a mixture of athletes remaining in all positions on the team, including the linebacker position.

During my first week of scrimmages, while playing weak-side line-backer, I remember tackling running back Walt Garrison. Walt got up and said, "Good hit, Jones." Man, I felt like a million. A few days later during the scrimmage session, Mike Ditka, a player coach, while playing tight end, did a crack-back block on me at knee level. Mike wasn't trying to intentionally hurt me with that block, but it was on the weakest part of my body—the part the doctor had forgotten to check during my exam. The crack-back block below the waist was legal in 1971 but has long since been ruled an illegal hit.

That hit by Mike would prove to be the beginning of the end of my pro aspirations. I never let on to the doctor just how bad my knee felt because I knew an exam would show that the ligaments had been damaged much earlier than that hit by Mike.

A couple of days later it was time for me to be timed in the forty-yard dash. I had practiced thrusting off and running with shoes and without shoes. I knew that my time would be higher due to the injury, but I had no choice but to run the forty as fast as I could. My time was 5.7 seconds—not fast enough for the coach to pay extra close attention in future practices, even though I excelled at my position.

One evening after practice, I had the opportunity to sit and talk briefly with All-Pro running back, C. Hill. Hill was the star running back with Dallas at the time. I had noticed the seven or eight rental cars that were parked on campus, so I asked Hill who the cars were for. He said that they were for the players to use, courtesy of the rental company. I asked him if he would be driving one. Hill responded without any anger in his voice, "Jones, those cars are for the white veteran players, not me."

My knee did not get any better during a two-week period. An agent would have held me out of practice and demanded time for rehabilitation, but I had no agent or anyone else to provide guidance. Long after my release, I realized that Dallas should not have released me while I was injured, but privileges were taken.

My short time with the Dallas Cowboys made me feel like I had gained ten years of experience about life and its disappointments.

I only had one private meeting with Coach Tom Landry while with the Cowboys. That meeting went like this: "Hey, Jones, I've watched you, and I think you can make this team. What I want you to do first is cut your hair." I had a large afro at the time. Coach Landry also informed me that he was a Christian. I got my hair cut that next day.

The year I was in camp was the year Roger Staubach and Craig Morton were vying for the starting job at quarterback. I was looking forward to my arrival at camp because Pettis Norman, a JCSU alumnus, was the starting tight end with Dallas. Prior to the start of that NFL season, Pettis was traded to the San Diego Chargers.

CHAPTER ELEVEN

I was quite sure that the condition of my knees had shortened my National Football League career, but I was also very sure my injured knees were responsible for my military medical deferment in 1968. This injury probably saved my life because it prevented me being drafted into the army and being shipped to Vietnam in 1968, the year of the Tat Offensive, an offensive that saw more than five thousand US soldiers killed.

I returned to Durham and my parents' home, where my wife Barbara and two-year-old daughter, Tara, were living. I was very pleased that I did not return to North Carolina empty-handed and without future plans.

While with the Cowboys, I had become aware that only a few of the rookies had obtained a college degree. I was one of only two African American rookie linebackers who had obtained a college degree.,

One of the rookies whom I befriended had played football at A & T State University in Greensboro, North Carolina. He had been offered a position at Lincoln University in Jefferson City, Missouri, but failed to get his degree during his last semester. Just in case I did not make the team, Dave had given me the phone number and contact's name at Lincoln so I could pursue the position of assistant director of student activities, the position he had planned to pursue but no longer could because he did not graduate.

Immediately upon my release from the Cowboys, I placed a call to the president of Lincoln University, from Coach Tubbs's office. During my brief phone call, I let the Lincoln University executive know that I was calling him from the office of Coach Tubbs', the linebacker coach of the Dallas Cowboys. After I explained that I was being released and how I had obtained his name and number, I no longer had to sell him on accepting me for the position of director of student activities at Lincoln.

Now all I had to do was get Barbara, Tara, and I to Jefferson City, Missouri, 1,024 miles away. I had to meet a deadline if I wanted the job in Jefferson City; therefore, I decided to try to talk Barbara into us hitching a U-Haul trailer to our 1957 VW and heading out for Jeff City, Missouri. A few days later, I had been successful in convincing Barbara to relocate halfway across the country.

We traveled those 1,024 miles, including over the Appalachian Mountains, without any problems. When I pulled the VW into the driveway of the home we had rented unseen, the clutch went totally out.

My mother later informed me about her vision of us going over a cliff in those mountains; therefore, she had prayed continuously for our safety. Barbara would tell me later that she was horrified about traveling that far from home in that VW, while towing a trailer that was larger than the car.

The God Spirit had watched over my family and me on this trip—the first of many times that I would attribute our safety and good fortune to this powerful spirit.

Jefferson City was the capital of Missouri. With a population of thirty two thousand, Jeff City had become the capital only because it was located in the middle of the state; half way between St Louis to the east and Kansas City to the west.

The student activities job was not a great one, so I had time to think about other things I wanted to do. Barbara had not yet begun her college studies. A short time after I began in my position, I was informed that Barbara and I could take classes free as long as I was employed by the university.

Barbara received her BA degree, and I received a master's degree in guidance and counseling and had compiled twenty-eight of the required thirty-two hours toward my master's degree in business ad-ministration before leaving the university's employment.

I worked, and we studied at Lincoln from 1971 until August of 1976. I served as director of student activities for three semesters. At the end of the third semester, I received a call from the university president. He asked me if I would attend a meeting of his fiscal staff that next day. Of course I accepted Dr. Daniels's invitation.

The next day at 10:00 a.m., I reported to Dr. Daniels's office, where the meeting was to be held. The meeting was called to order, and the first order of business was a report on the embarrassing fis-cal and management condition of the Lincoln University bookstore.

The manager was in the fall of his life, and the student workers were running the bookstore. The store had averaged losing more than $25,000 per semester during the past four semesters, and the president was on the spot to somehow improve the management efficiencies and eliminate the financial losses at the university bookstore.

Dr. Daniels turned to me and commented, "Mr. Jones, I want you to assume the management duties of the Lincoln University bookstore immediately and make it a profitable operation. Will you accept the challenge?"

I was shocked and elated at the same time. I was totally unchallenged in my present position and wanted—needed—something more challenging. I think I gave my positive response to Dr. Daniels's question within fifteen to twenty seconds after his request.

Later in the day I received a call from Dr. Daniels. He wanted to let me know that the university was depending on me to turn the store operations around, and whatever I needed to get the job done, he would see that I received it.

The next morning Dr. Daniels accompanied me to the bookstore, which was on the second floor of the student union building, a floor above my student activities office.

I had visited the bookstore on numerous occasions and had met the elderly gentleman who was the manager. I had also met the part-time student employees. During the months while working as director of student activities, I had been privy to numerous conversations about how the student employees were selling books taken from the bookstore.

The manager quickly let me know that he was relieved that I was assuming his duties because he had wanted to retire for two years.

The only other full-time adult employed in the store was Betty, the secretary/cashier. Betty was a white female in her late forties.

I knew I would need to be creative if the bookstore was to become a profitable venture; while at the same time, greatly improving the services to the students and faculty. One of my ventures was to begin stocking used books for sale to students. I figured by providing the students used books to purchase, they could save up to fifty percent.

My research had lead me to the National Association of College Stores, (NACS) organization; the largest used book reseller in the nation. I remember travelling to Lincoln, Nebraska on a fall Saturday morning to make a major book purchase. As I entered the city limits of Lincoln, I began to notice that everyone were wearing red. By the time I reached the center of the city, there were thousands and thousands of people walking the streets; all wearing red. While refueling, the station attendant informed me that the Nebraska Cornhuskers were playing their rivals, the Oklahoma Sooners down at the stadium, at 1:00 PM.

I was able to meet with the manager of the NACS and was given a tour of the 32,000 square foot used book facility. I knew right away that I had found a gold mine for Lincoln University, its students, and faculty.

Travelling in rural Missouri, Nebraska and Kansas, during the early to mid nineteen seventies, only a few radio station were available. Those stations that had reception played country music. Within two years, I had become a fan of country music; with a steady dose of George Jones, Lee Greenwood, Randy Travis and others. I found this music to be quite enjoyable and easy listening while on the road.

There were a number of interesting and unique thing about Lincoln University, Jefferson City:

1. It was the only Land Grant College in Missouri, established to educate African Americans.
2. When I arrived at Lincoln, the student enrollment was approximately 60 percent white and 40 percent black. The faculty was approximately 65 percent white and 35 percent black.
3. All the white students were local and used Lincoln University as a community college. No white student lived on campus. The black students were mostly from Kansas City, St Louis, Chicago, and a few other large Midwest and numerous East Coast cities.

My first order of business was a staff meeting where I announced the changes that had taken place, and that I had accepted the position of manager of the bookstore. I quickly informed the staff that all part-time employees and the one full-time employee would retain their jobs, unless there were those who wanted to or thought they needed to resign.

I had to be quite blunt during this meeting because I already knew that at least three of the student workers were removing books and supplies from the store and selling these products to other students.

Betty was an excellent employee. She assisted me in purging the staff of the student workers who had to be removed. With a lot of hard work, good student employees, and good fiscal controls, the store turned a profit in my first year as manager. The faculty and students were pleased also because the store was stocked with all of the books and supplies needed and required by students and faculty at the beginning of each semester for the first time. I operated the store for approximately three years and seven months.

CHAPTER TWELVE

I n December of 1975, I distributed my resume to major corporations throughout the United States. Within three months, I had accepted interview offers from five major firms: General Motors, Ford,
Osco Drugs, Standard Oil, and IBM Corporation. I was offered positions with four of these firms.

Even though I had not submitted a resume to US Steel Corporation,
this was the corporation with which Barbara and I finally agreed to
accept a position. We decided on US Steel because of the numerous
special circumstances and opportunities involved in employment.

How the opportunity with US Steel happened is another one of
those hard-to-explain occurrences. The Lincoln University bookstore
was located on the second floor of the University's student union
building. The university had invited numerous large and small businesses to visit the campus and interview seniors for jobs. The businesses were provided space on the third floor of the student union
building, where they had space to interview interested students.

Students had appointments for five-minute sessions with the firms in which they were interested.

On this special day, I left the bookstore and, for reasons not known, walked up to the third floor of the student union. As I reached the third floor, I saw this black stranger standing approximately ten feet away. I spoke, and he responded.

He then asked if I was there for an interview. I responded no, that I was manager of the university bookstore. He introduced himself, and after a brief conversation, he informed me that he was waiting for a student to arrive for his five-minute interview. The scheduled student did not arrive, and our conversation continued for the next five minutes.

He then informed me that he was recruiting for US Steel Corporation. He said it appeared that I could be the person for whom he had been searching. He asked if I would be interested in an out-side sales position with the US Steel Corporation. He continued by informing me that US Steel was searching for an African American to serve in the position of outside sales engineer. I would be the first outside sales person of color in the history of the company. That person would need to have the personality, interpersonal skills, and pro-fessional skills to interact and matriculate in the country club and business atmosphere and communicate effectively with company executives and executives of the firm's customers and clients. The gentleman said that he was pretty sure I was that person, if I was interested.

He asked if I would be willing to fly to Pittsburgh, PA, to inter-view at the US Steel headquarters; if so, he would send me an airline ticket within seven days. He said that there were no strings attached. At worst, I would take time from my schedule to travel to and from

Pittsburgh, and the positives would be an opportunity to meet and interview with vice presidents of a major corporation and to visit Pittsburgh, Pennsylvania.

I accepted his offer and traveled to Pittsburgh and interviewed with six vice presidents of US Steel Corporation in one day. At the end of the interview sessions, I met the vice president of personnel and was offered the position of management trainee, the position prior to becoming an outside sales representative, if I passed their "tests."

My salary as bookstore manager at Lincoln was $7,800. You can imagine the energy that surged through my body when Vice President Ralph offered me a starting salary of $15,000 while completing my eight months of special training. In addition to the $15,000, as an outside sales rep, I would have a very attractive benefit plan, expense account, and company car.

It was all that I could do not to jump out of my seat with joy; but I knew that I had to keep my composure. After all, the recruiter had informed me that, if successful, I would become the first African American to hold the position of outside sales representative for the US Steel Corporation, the largest steel firm in the nation.

After managing to stay in my seat and keep my composure, I informed Mr. Ralph that I felt that this was an acceptable offer, but I would need to discuss the offer with my wife prior to giving a final answer. It was very apparent that my response impressed Mr. Ralph. He responded, "Take the time you need to make a decision, Jones." To make the offer even more attractive, he stated that if I did decide to accept, I would have the option of deciding at which of the approximately seven steel mills in the country to receive my eight months of training.

I could barely wait to tell Barbara the great news about US Steel's offer. Of the five offers I had in hand as a result of my interviews, US Steel's offer matched the highest financially and exceeded all others in special opportunities.

After Barbara and I discussed the pros and cons of the various offers, I knew that I would accept the offer from US Steel for one specific reason in addition to the salary offer: I wanted to become the first African American in the company's history to serve as an outside sales representative'.

Mr. Ralph and the US Steel executives were pleased that I decided to come on board. After doing some research, I decided to use the Lorain, Ohio, works as my home base during my special training. Lorain Works was only twenty-six miles west of Cleveland, Ohio, and Cleveland was where US Steel housed one of its district sales offices.

CHAPTER THIRTEEN

I clearly remember saying to Barbara in the early 1970s while travelling from Durham, North Carolina, to Jefferson City, Missouri, while employed at Lincoln University, "Ohio is one state in which I would prefer not to live." Less than five years later, Ohio was now the state in which I had agreed to accept employment with US Steel Corporation. This decision was made because the US Steel Lorain Works and its Cleveland district sales office were the best profit centers in the corporation.

On August 3, 1976, I left Barbara and Tara behind in Jeff City and drove my Orange VW Super Beetle the 670 miles to Lorain, Ohio. After the approximate ten-hour trip, I arrived at the Holiday Inn at the Midway Mall. The mall was located between Elyria and Lorain, Ohio. The temperature the night of my arrival dipped to forty-nine degrees, on August fourth!

The next morning I woke up early in anticipation of the beginning of our (my family's and my) new life in a "foreign land." I had breakfast and departed for the US Steel Corporation's Lorain Works, approximately three miles north and less than three miles from Lake Erie. Twenty miles across Lake Erie lay the country of Canada, a foreign nation.

I will never forget, as long as I live, my unique experiences during that three-mile trip to the mill. Approximately two miles into the trip I began to notice a smell similar to rotten eggs. I also noticed what appeared to be particles in the atmosphere. As soon as I turned from Route 57, left on to 28th Street, where the US Steel Lorain Works was located, the rotten-egg smell was at its peak, and due to the particles in the air, I could only see approximately two hundred to three hundred feet ahead of me. This was my introduction to the steel industry and the condition of the cities where these steel production facilities were located.

In 1976, Lorain Works of US Steel employed a little more than twelve thousand well-paid citizens from the surrounding areas. I arrived at the visitors' parking lot and asked the guard for directions to the management offices. He pointed to a three-story building that appeared to be more than one hundred years old.

I entered the building, and the plant superintendent's executive assistant welcomed me with a smile. She led me to her boss's office, that of Mr. Don Pass, plant superintendent. I was left in the care and guidance of Mr. Pass for approximately forty-five minutes as he welcomed me to his plant. He then introduced me to the plant's director of operations.

When I dressed for the day, I had no idea what to expect. If I had, I surely would not have worn my light-tan three-piece suit. Even though before taking a tour of the massive steel complex, which took up approximately two miles along 28th Street, I was provided a safety hat and glasses, steel-toed shoes, and a green fire-retardant jacket.

The tour took approximately four hours, starting from the finishing end of the mill and ending with the blast furnace and where the raw materials entered the plant. The tour was quite frightening. Experiencing this type of dirty and dangerous work environment, especially after being employed on a college campus, was quite depressing.

By the time the tour was over, I was sick from breathing the various fumes, especially the sulfur gasses. Needless to say, the tan suit was never to be worn again. The major question staring at me now was: Have I made a serious mistake accepting this position with US Steel Corporation?

I knew that I was a special project for US Steel by the special attention given to me by everyone, including Mr. Pass. He reviewed the plans that had been laid out for me, including my extensive eight-week training session at the US Steel headquarters in Pittsburgh.

I was temporarily assigned to the superintendent of production planning, one of the cleanest areas in the plant. I would be there only three weeks before an eight-week session of my special training began in the US Steel headquarters building in Pittsburgh.

CHAPTER FOURTEEN

Upon arriving in Pittsburgh, I checked in to the William Penn Hotel, the hotel where all US Steel employees visiting the headquarters stayed. The building appeared to be more than one hundred years old and was known for its spacious and beautiful rooms. I was quite impressed until I arrived at my room. As I opened the door, I almost fell over the bed. I quickly realized that I would not be staying in the section where the paying guests were staying.

That evening the company held a reception for the fifteen sales trainees scheduled for this training session. As I entered the room where the reception was being held, I immediately saw another black face staring back at me. I introduced myself as I met each trainee, while making my way over to introduce myself to this other black face. As I approached Mike, he began to smile, and we did our special handshake and spent probably six or seven minutes talking. We agreed to meet after the reception, so we both proceeded to meet the other thirteen white trainees.

Mike and I met after the reception and conversed for a couple of hours. He was from Chicago, the Hyde Park community. Of course, he had never heard of Lorain County or the city of Lorain or Elyria, Ohio. Before arriving on August fourth, I had never heard of Elyria or Lorain County either. I knew that the steel mill was in Lorain, Ohio, and that Lorain was close to Cleveland, Ohio, and also close to Oberlin, Ohio, and Oberlin College.

Mike and I both knew why we were in this special training session, and we became good friends—not just because we were the only two African American trainees, but also because we actually liked each other.

The training classes began the next morning at 8:00 a.m. sharp. The trainer was a middle-aged white male. He attempted to be as comfortable with this class of trainees as in the past, but Mike and I could tell that he was well aware that this class was different from any other he had taught.

After the training session was over for the day, the trainer decided that he would give some information and guidance about the hotel and the surrounding areas—where to go and where not to go. His guidance was pretty straightforward until he made the comment, "There are many places you guys can go in Pittsburgh and be safe, but whatever you do, don't go up to the hill district." After realizing the comment he had made, his eyes glanced directly toward the area where Mike and I were sitting.

Only the two of us determined immediately why he had made this comment. As we would confirm later, we both knew immediately that the hill district had to be the area where blacks lived in Pittsburgh. He was well aware that Mike and I knew why he had made this comment, but we did not expose him at that time.

The classes were Monday morning until Friday at 4:00 p.m. We were free to do as we pleased after 4:00 p.m. daily. The first place Mike and I explored was the "hill." Sure enough, the hill was a black community. During our eight weeks in Pittsburgh, we became well known at the YMCA on the hill, where we both played basketball at least twice weekly. Mike was an All-State player in high school, and so was I.

Many of the guys would inquire about our whereabouts because they had not seen us the prior afternoon. We took great pride in telling them that we had been up on the hill! They eventually realized that black people lived in the hill district.

Most weekends I would travel the 150 miles back to Elyria to be with my family. Chicago was a little too far for Mike to travel for the weekend, so he remained in Pittsburgh. I invited him, and he did accompany me to Elyria on a couple of weekends.

During the eight-week session, I became friends with a number of the trainees. One of the trainees was from South Carolina. After having a couple of drinks one evening, he decided that he would inform the group that this was the first time he had spent so much time with black people. He went on to say that his father was a racist—so much so that his favorite TV show was "The Price is Right," and whenever a black contestant would win, his father would become extremely angry and turn the TV off. I think Mike and I were pleased that this son of a racist could share this with us. Of course, we had already observed that he had some of his father traits. In this case, the fruit had not fallen far from the tree.

I am pleased to say that one of the trainees in this class has been a good neighbor of mine in Elyria for more than seventeen years.

After the Pittsburgh training session, we traveled to Chicago, where we trained for an additional two weeks. This was Mike's hometown, so he, being a bachelor, invited me to stay with him. Hyde Park was home for Mike—a beautiful well-kept area, the area where the first African American President of the United States would reside and meet the beautiful woman who would become his wife. By this time, all of the trainees were tired of training sessions and were glad they had come to, hopefully, a successful end of "the beginning."

CHAPTER FIFTEEN

After these training sessions, it was extremely hard to return permanently to the steel-mill environment. Little did I know that Mr. Pass and the management of US Steel had some immediate plans for me that would not only delay my return to the mill but would start me on a journey I never could have imagined.

After a few days back in the mill, Mr. Pass called me into his office and informed me that he would appreciate if I would serve as US Steel's loaned executive for the United Way of Greater Lorain County's fund-raising campaign. Of course, I accepted this offer because I felt this would be an excellent opportunity to see Lorain County and delay my assuming my responsibilities in the mill.

I had no idea just how prestigious it was to serve as a "Loaned Executive for the United Way." I can now confirm that my serving as the loaned executive provided me the valuable opportunities to begin my interactions with the major business, civic, and political leaders in the county. I served in this capacity for six exciting and informative weeks.

Being the first African American to serve as a loaned executive for the United Way was highlighted by both the United Way executives and US Steel executives.

After a week of training with other loaned executives and my inside assistant, I was ready to begin my visits and meetings with the businesses and corporations that had been arranged by my inside assistant.

My approximately thirty-minute session with the management and employees consisted of a six- to eight-minute speech, a seven-minute video by Loretta Lynn, titled "If You Don't Do It, It won't Get Done." After approximately fifteen showings of Loretta Lynn, I began to become addicted to her West Virginia twang. My brief pitch and Loretta's pitch for the United Way helped the donations by the business community to exceed all prior years' giving.

In those six weeks, I met many of the movers and shakers in Lorain County and northern Ohio. I didn't know it at that time, but I had met and impressed two powerful Republicans: Mr. Eric T Nord, president and chairman of Nordson Corporation and Attorney Scribner L. Fauver, managing partner of Fauver, Tattersal & Gallagher Law Firm and former state representative. These two powerful men would play major roles in my future.

That year the United Way campaign was a great success financially, and the social celebration was one of the highlights of the year. My United Way duties had ended successfully, and now there was nothing else keeping me from my full-time duties in the Lorain Works of US Steel.

CHAPTER SIXTEEN

I must now focus on the business for which I moved to Lorain County, Ohio. Once my two training classes were over, I returned to Jeff City to bring my family to Lorain County. I was totally impressed that US Steel had agreed to hire professional movers to transport our belongings to our new home city. I had described the condition of the air surrounding the mill to Barbara; therefore, we decided not to look for housing in the city of Lorain. We finally decided to rent a town house in Elyria, across from the Lorain County Community College (LCCC) campus. I will share information about my special relationship with LCCC later.

Upon returning to the mill, I was informed that as a management trainee, I was allowed to drive into the mill and use the appropriate management parking spaces. At first it appeared that no one seemed to care that I owned an orange Volkswagen Super Beetle until I began driving it into the mill on a daily basis. Union personnel had to park outside of the mill.

After approximately four weeks of driving my orange foreign-made vehicle the length of the mill to arrive at the production planning office, I was called into the manager's office for a meeting. I had no idea why this meeting was being called, but I was sure it wasn't for anything negative that I had done. After a couple of minutes into the meeting, it became clear to me that whatever the subject, my manager was having a difficult time discussing it with me. He was having a hard time communicating the issue because this was his first time supervising an African American trainee. It was apparent that this experience wasn't easy for him, but his secretary rescued him. It appeared that she had interacted with blacks outside of her work environment. After Bill's secretary intervened, he was able to hold a chitchat with me but did not discuss what he had planned.

My manager never got around to telling me what he really called me into his office to tell me that day. It was approximately four days later when Skip, the production foreman, called me to the side and informed me of the problem. Skip was a "good old boy" who had taken a liking to me and had spent hours talking—talking about any and everything. He wanted me to know that he understood the importance of my presence.

Skip informed me that the management was very concerned about me driving my orange Super Beetle into the plant. It appeared that half of Skip's vocabulary was curse words. After Skip provided the full story, I was grateful to him for alerting me of the possible dangers.

The American steel industry was suffering because foreign steel firms were producing and delivering their steel products to the Cleveland docks at prices less than what the US mills could produce their steel products for. The unions, management, and the entire nation were convinced that these foreign mills were dumping steel into the United States, and anger was rampant.

Skip informed me that management felt I was in danger because I was driving this bright-orange foreign car right into the plant on a daily basis. He had mentioned it in passing once before, but this time I clearly understood the danger. From that day on, I would park my orange VW outside of the plant.

CHAPTER SEVENTEEN

After arriving in Lorain County, Barbara was kept busy during the first three months unpacking, furnishing the apartment, and enrolling Tara in her new school. She was extremely pleased that she had obtained her bachelor's degree while I had worked at Lincoln. At the same time, she was also disappointed that she was not able to take advantage of the four-year scholarship that had been offered to her by St. Louis University.

The weather in Missouri had the coldest temperatures we had experienced—until now. I had read about the snowfall amounts in Cleveland, but that had not prepared us for the winter weather we would experience during our first year.

We experienced our first snowfall October 14, 1976. We thought the snow was beautiful, but that snowfall in October would be the start of a continual snowfall until March 1977. I remember walking out of the town house and attempting to take a breath through my mouth, and the cold literally took my breath away. By early February

1977, there were mountains of snow everywhere because the temperatures had seldom risen above freezing during that five-month period.

Just when we thought we had lived through the harshest of that winter, a monster snowstorm hit us in late February. The storm lasted for three days and was so severe, thousands of motorists were snowbound for days. One big rig trucker stopped on Interstate 80 to wait for the storm to subside, but it didn't for two and a half days. The snow completely covered his rig for approximately five days until the snowplow drivers located him. He survived by eating snow and what little food he had in his rig.

Barbara was not happy that I had convinced the family to come to this deep freeze. At times I was not sure if she would stay in Lorain County or return to North Carolina. She stuck it out, and we survived the winter of 1977.

CHAPTER EIGHTEEN

I was close to completing my sales training after approximately six months in the mill. I felt that I had gained the knowledge necessary to be promoted to the position of outside sales engineer. My manager was aware that I had become bored and needed something to keep me interested or at least occupied until that promotion actually happened.

Somehow a number of the gigantic three-ton steel billets were coming up missing from the billet yard each month, and no one knew what was happening to these massive pieces of steel. My manager explained the problem and asked if I could focus on an answer for the missing billets problem. I am not sure if he really thought that I could solve this problem or if he gave me the project because he knew that I was bored.

I was very pleased to focus my attention on this project, especially after being told the value of these billets. One thing had become very clear to me during those first six months in the mill: there were dozens of different nationalities of people working in this mill of twelve thousand employees. Many of these employees either could not speak English or could only speak broken English.

I had encountered a number of union and management employees who had shown their disdain for me—either by words or expressions and stares.

I knew that I had to be careful while attempting to find the answer to the missing billets. The word was that these billets were being removed from the plant and sold. I was not interested in being a detective; I just wanted to get some answers without any confrontations. I knew that I could not go around asking questions of union workers or management workers, but I felt that I had to find a way to solve this billet problem.

At the time, the mill had very little automation, but I heard that Lorain County Community College (LCCC) had a computer programming class. What if I could have a computer program developed that would keep track of the billets in the billet yard? I presented my idea to my manager, and he did not completely understand my plan but gave me the go-ahead anyway.

I was able to have this simple program developed within a couple of weeks. I loaded it on my home PC and practiced for a couple of days until I was familiar with its operations. I then presented the program to my manager and showed him how it would keep track of the billets produced and the billet stored in the billet yards. He was impressed and told me to proceed with my plan.

Now came the hard part: getting the foremen and union leaders to accept my program and install it on their systems. My manager called a special meeting of foremen and union personnel, and

I explained the software program and demonstrated its capabilities. My software program was not received very well by the foremen or the union personnel for two reasons: (1) most were computer illiterate, and (2) they did not want this PC program spying on what they were doing. Both groups were well aware that if they rejected this project, it would appear as though they did not want to help save the company money that it was losing.

A few days after the meeting, my manager informed me that both the union and the foremen had agreed to have the program installed in production planning and at the billet yard. Now my job was to train the foremen and their union assistants who worked in and supervised the billet yard operations. This training would require me to enter the mill at the beginning of each shift.

On my first morning of training, I arrived early and parked my orange Super Beetle in the lot outside of the plant, at the lower East 28th Street entrance. I sat in my car and watched the union employees walk and meander their way from their vehicles to the mill entrance. Most were acting as though they had left their minds in their vehicle or at home. After a while, I noticed that many of the employees, prior to arriving at the mill entrance, were stopping at a building approximately hundred yards across the street from the mill entrance.

I exited my car and decided to explore the building. This building housed a bar. What I saw left me speechless. These mill employees, prior to entering the mill to work in many dangerous areas, were having their regular morning shot of alcohol! I could tell that their morning visits had become a ritual because for many of the workers the bartender already had their drinks placed on the bar when they arrived. I didn't observe anyone having more than one drink. The average time these employees spent in the bar was three to five minutes.

What do I do with this information? Am I the only one who is aware of this dangerous practice? Should I inform my manager? These and many other questions were filling my mind. I quickly realized that it was all but impossible for some of the managers not to know about this practice; therefore, I made an executive decision that it was not my responsibility to report the behavior of these employees.

My first training session began on time, and from the attitude and actions of the first two participants, I knew that this would be a hard lesson to teach. I taught a total of eight employees how to use the PC billet-tracking program.

After my in-office training sessions were completed, I had to visit each area of the plant where the software program was being used. One morning while on my way to visit the billet yard, I noticed there was someone in the massive, magnetic overhead crane. These massive cranes had the capacity to pick up twenty tons of steel at a time and move these massive loads from the holding and cooling areas to the various stocking yards.

Skip had warned me about the dangers of the billet yard, so that morning I knew that I had to be extremely careful while entering the yard because these guys had clearly shown me that they did not want to see this software program installed.

I knew the crane operator saw me approaching, and when I was approximately fifty yards away from the crane, the operator "accidentally" dropped the twenty tons of billets to the ground from approximately fifteen feet in the air. The extremely loud noise and dust left me frozen in my tracks. Fear overwhelmed me, but once I could move and see the crane operator, we stared silently for at least ten seconds. From the appearance of his stare, prior to asking if I was all right, he confirmed that the dropping of the steel had been intentional.

His actions were intended to send me a clear message: that this project had put me in a position where an intentional accident could happen, while working in a dangerous environment. This magnetic crane warning alerted me that deadly "accidents" could happen to me at any time.

From that morning forward, I never again visited the foremen or their union assistants in the plant operations area of the mill. I would receive their reports in the production planning office area, and whatever reports they submitted, the same would be submitted to the production planning manager.

I never informed my manager about what had happened that morning—the morning when I decided that my life was much more important than any attempt to solve a missing billet problem. When I finally departed the mill a few months later, my program was still being used. I have no idea if the program corrected the missing billet problem or if the software program was used to cover up the billet problem.

CHAPTER NINETEEN

Within a few months after my family settled in Elyria, I knew that it would be important to meet as many members of the black community as possible. My job activities had put me in contact with very few blacks, even while serving as the loaned executive for the United Way.

Barbara and I knew that the best way to meet our people was to attend some of the churches in Lorain and Elyria. I can assure you this was not the most important reason to attend church. Our main reason was to thank God for our blessings and to ask for guidance in this foreign land.

In my position with US Steel, I had been able to meet many of the white business, civic, and political leaders. It became very clear that there were very few blacks who were included in the civic and political power base of Lorain County, and that there were no mainstream black-owned businesses.

In the mid-1970s, Lorain County was thriving economically. A county of less than three hundred thousand citizens was home to numerous major employers: US Steel, (twelve thousand employees); Ford Motor Company, two plants (ten thousand employees); General Motors (three thousand employees); Nordson, American Ship Building, TRW, and many smaller firms.

Income levels were high enough for the area to be listed in the *Wall Street Journal* as one of the top ten counties nationally for workers' salaries and family income. This present financial condition provided a false sense of security for a population where an extremely large number of its citizens did not have a high school education. To secure an excellent paying job at most of the corporations, a high school education was not required. Little did these citizens know that a major economic downturn was less than five years away.

The great salaries, including salaries of blacks and Hispanics, had blinded all but a few to the racism and discrimination that overtly and covertly existed in the county. Most African Americans' and Hispanics' lack of attention to the racism and discrimination in the county greatly decreased the obvious need to become involved in or support the activities of the NAACP or other civil-rights organizations.

Having been raised in the south, I could clearly see the racism in Lorain County that very few other African American could see or wanted to see. Although different from the racism of the south, this was a sophisticated kind of racism, but it was still racism. It was so clear to me because of my numerous experiences early in life: born and raised in the south, parents owning land, my brief time with the Dallas Cowboys, and my experiences while at Lincoln University.

I had already learned to live in two worlds: the white world and the black one. Living in both worlds had become quite easy. I was very comfortable and proud to be an African American and was eager to matriculate in the white world because that was where my business future lay.

As I associated with and communicated with the African American communities, I became very aware that the black leaders were concerned about me coming in and disrupting their community power bases. The more they knew about me, the more they feared me and attempted to shut my family and me out of their activities.

Just about the time I was ready to abandon the black community altogether, a breakthrough came. There had been talk of bringing an Urban League chapter to Lorain County, but no one knew exactly how to make this happen. My wife Barbara had been attending community meetings, and the topic had been how to establish an Urban League chapter in the county. One evening, Barbara could not attend the community meeting being held at the Holiday Inn, and she asked if I would attend.

I attended this meeting and did a lot of listening and had the pleasure of meeting Mrs. Dorothy Anderson, a leader and community activist and wife of the only African American medical doctor in the county. Mrs. Anderson was a very attractive light-skinned lady in her early forties. When she spoke at this meeting, people listened. Although I could tell Mrs. Anderson's experiences, as they related to the business community, were quite limited, I was sure that we would be able to develop a good working relationship, and we did.

I was beginning to see a pattern developing as I became more and more familiar with the African American community in Lorain County. Lorain County was the next county west of Cuyahoga County (the largest county in Ohio), meandering along the shores of Lake Erie.

The African American population in the two counties was as different as night and day. The city of Cleveland (the largest city in Ohio at that time) was located in Cuyahoga County. Cleveland had a few very active and progressive African American communities and numerous citywide leaders: Mayor Carl Stokes, his brother, Louis Stokes (who would later become a US Congressman), city council president George Forbes, and a number of other leaders.

Lorain County was a totally different story. There were a few African Americans serving as members of the city council in Elyria and Lorain. (I will provide more on the role these leaders played in shaping the image of Lorain County later.)

It is an extremely dangerous situation when racial discrimination is running rampant in your county, and your community leaders appear to have blinders on.

In the early 1990s, I began referring to Lorain County as Slorain County because of the backward thinking, the racism and the discrimination that existed, and the lack of effective leadership in the African American and Hispanic communities.

Dorothy Anderson chaired the minority community meetings and after my third meeting, the committee decided to invite the regional director of the National Urban League to the meeting. Mr. Ernie Cooper traveled from Chicago to meet with the committee members.

Ernie was impressed with the committee's planning and organization and returned to Chicago to provide the powers that be his recommendations about the feasibility of an Urban League chapter in Lorain County. Within three weeks, Mr. Cooper returned to Lorain County for his second meeting. The update centered on two major questions: (1) Why did Lorain County need an Urban League

Chapter when the Cleveland chapter was so close? (2) How would this chapter support itself financially?

I knew that these questions would be asked because Mr. Cooper had called me a week or so prior to his second visit. He had researched the backgrounds of the persons on the committee, and I was the only person on the committee with a direct financial and business connection to the corporate community in the county. The corporate connection he saw was my employment with US Steel Corporation.

My travels throughout Lorain County as a loaned executive had afforded me the opportunity to meet and impress a number of powerful businessmen in the county. Two of these men were Eric T Nord, chairman and CEO of Nordson Corporation and Scribner L. Fauver, former state representative and partner in one of the largest law firms in the county. At the time, I could not have imagined the critical role these two men would play in my future—personally, businesswise, and in the civic realm.

Ernie made it very clear: if he could not see an ongoing stream of financial support, a chapter would not be approved for Lorain County.

I only met Eric Nord a couple of brief times when I made my United Way presentation and at the United Way campaign dinner. After the dinner Eric pulled me to the side and informed me that he was very impressed with my business and civic focus, and that we should stay in touch.

Prior to the Urban League opportunity, I had no reason to communicate with Mr. Nord, but I knew this was my opportunity to bring two foreign factions—African Americans businesspeople—of Lorain County together for the first time and in a unique and powerful way.

Prior to my coming to Lorain County, there had been no African American businessperson who had dared to enter into the business and corporate world of Lorain County. Whites and blacks did not socialize together unless there was a political function.

Whites did their thing, and blacks did theirs, and seldom did they get together. Therefore, neither group really knew the needs or thoughts of the other. Each just assumed that it knew the other. It wasn't just the blacks not associating with the whites; the blacks in Elyria and Lorain were not talking to each other, and the blacks in Oberlin weren't communicating with Elyria or Lorain. Lorain County was a mess, and Ernie had become somewhat aware of these issues. He also realized that each city—Elyria, Lorain, and Oberlin—had their separate NAACP chapters, and they seldom communicated with each other.

Knowing I did not have the finances and knowing that Mrs. Anderson was the only person on the committee with some extra funds, I decided to schedule a meeting with Eric Nord to discuss his feelings and thoughts about creating an Urban League chapter in the county. From my brief meetings with Mr. Nord, I was aware of his philanthropic nature and giving through the Nordson Foundation. This was a foundation started by him and his brother Evan; therefore, I felt pretty comfortable presenting the Urban League opportunity to him.

Eric and I met, and he was eager to know more about the league and what the league's focus would be in Lorain County. I provided all of the information I could and then suggested that he and I meet with Ernie Cooper. Ernie was elated to meet with Eric, was able to answer all of Eric's questions, and provided a draft for a three-year operating budget.

Eric committed himself to assisting financially to establish an Urban League chapter in Lorain County.

As an introduction and a bridge to provide financial support for the league, Eric called a meeting of the business and civic leaders of Lorain County. The breakfast meeting was held at DeLucas Place in the Park, a facility with a four-hundred-person capacity. The 7:30 a.m. meeting was held on February 2, 1978. More than two inches of snow had fallen the night before.

I awoke and looked out my bedroom window, and a chill traveled down my spine. Had all the planning and invitations for this meeting been for naught? We had two inches of snow on the ground. I arrived at DeLucas early and made sure that everything was in order.

I was truly amazed at 7:30 a.m. when the program was scheduled to begin and four hundred-plus businesspersons, civic leaders, and politicians were in their seats. I had never experienced anything like this in my lifetime. That morning I began to realize the power of this very humble man named Eric T. Nord. More than four hundred leaders in Lorain County had arrived for a breakfast meeting to hear about an organization that most had never heard of. They came because Eric Nord had requested their presence.

The Lorain County Urban League was born on that snowy morning in February 1978. This was the beginning of my personal relationship with Eric that would last for more than twenty tears. There were a couple of promises I had to make to Eric for his support of the league: (a) I would agree to serve as the league's board chairman, and (b) I would agree to head the search committee that would bring aboard the league's first president.

An Urban-League-trained president was not easy to find. The salary range was not very appealing, and Lorain County was an unknown entity to most who were qualified for the position. Finally, after Ernie realized that we would not be able to lure a seasoned veteran to lead the chapter, he gave us permission to hire a young man who he knew had some league experience and who was presently working in the Akron, Ohio, Urban League. We had to agree to send this young man to Urban League training sessions immediately upon his hiring.

The citizens' committee—Eric, Dorothy, and I—were well aware of how important it would be for the first league's board of directors to represent the makeup of the different communities. The first board of directors included: Larry D. Jones (board chair); Eric Nord, chair and CEO, Nordson Corporation; Scribner Fauver, partner, Fauver, Tattersal & Gallagher; Ben Norton, president of Lorain Products; Emma Mason, executive VP, Lorain National Bank; Dorothy Anderson, community leader; William S Wheatley, minister and community leader; William McCray, attorney; Jeptha Carroll, director of Nord Foundation; Juan Ortiz, director, El Centro; and a number of other community leaders throughout the African American, Hispanic, and white communities.

I would serve as chairman of the board of the league for twelve years—not of my own choosing but because of the constant struggles of the league financially and in an effort to increase community support. As I mentioned earlier, good paying jobs are the major reasons African Americans and Hispanics had not seen the need for an Urban League chapter in Lorain County, but by 1982 a great number of those jobs in Lorain County no longer existed.

The league's first office was out on State Route 254, on the border of the Elyria/Lorain city lines. The board decided to house the league there to display to the two largest cities that this was a new agency dedicated to serving the entire county.

CHAPTER TWENTY

Reverend William S. Wheatley and his wife, Geneva, and daughter, Angela Wheatley, relocated to Lorain County in 1976 to pastor at Jones Chapel African Methodist Episcopal Church, the church we eventually joined.

The Wheatleys and my family became very good friends. He was an excellent minister and a powerful community leader while he journeyed those twelve years in Elyria. I remember how we worked extremely well together as a voice between the black community and the businesspeople and political leaders and between the city and county law-enforcement agencies.

The last big project Wheatley and I worked on together was the major political campaign that pitted a Democrat against a Republican for Lorain County Prosecutor. The Democratic candidate was Dan Stringer, a local attorney, and the Republican candidate was an ex-Marine named Gregory White. This would be the first political office to be held by either candidate. Wheatley and I and many in the community had become aware of the anti-minority reputation of the Republican candidate, so we put our support behind Dan Stringer.

We knew the importance of having someone heading the county prosecutor's office who was sensitive in the treatment of the county's African American and Hispanic citizens. It didn't take long before we were holding meetings in the undercroft of Jones Chapel in support of Daniel Stringer because he had promised to be fair in his treatment of the minority population in Lorain County. Gregory White refused to make any promises to the minority community; as a matter of fact, he did not meet with any minority groups.

This would become a very close, hard-fought campaign, but in the end, we were disappointed because Gregory White defeated Stringer, and he achieved this without the support of the African American or the Hispanic vote. We were quite sure that this Republican victory would make it extremely hard for any progress to be made in the office of the prosecutor's treatment of African American and Hispanics. For twenty years Prosecutor White ruled Lorain County with an iron fist. Lawyers and judges feared White, and African Americans and Hispanics, especially their leaders, were targeted, and numerous lives were destroyed by the uneven and heavy-handed actions of Prosecutor White.

⟞⟜ ⟛⟝

The Urban League of Lorain County had an extremely slow beginning in the county. The leadership of the NAACP chapters did not want the league to be successful because of jealously and fear—fear that the league would make their agendas less important. The league and the NAACP were focused in two different areas (NAACP on social issues; the league, on jobs and housing), but that did not stop the invisible fighting and spreading of negative and harmful comments about the league by the NAACP executives and members.

At the league's annual dinners over the years, the white leadership attended because Eric Nord continued to support the league, and the African American and Hispanic/Latino leadership attended mostly because they wanted to be associated with this highly viable organization. The league received very little grass-roots community support during the first eight years in business. This support was still absent even after the league had achieved many successes in the areas of jobs and housing discrimination.

When I think about the many organizations of which I was a board member or chair, I have many regrets serving as chair of the league. Most of the regrets were because I could not say no to serving on the boards of twenty-eight important organizations over an eighteen-year period. Many of these organizations had never had African American or Hispanic/Latino representation; therefore, at the time, I felt it my duty to represent. In or around 1998, while I was hurrying down State Route 57 from a meeting in Elyria to another meeting in Lorain, I suddenly realized that I could no longer be all things to all people. I had been neglecting my family and some of my US Steel responsibilities in order to serve on these many boards. That next day I resigned from five of those eight boards.

⊨⊰ ⊱⊨

DAMN YOU, WILLIE LYNCH

After approximately fourteen years, I had come to the realization that I could no longer live my life committed to helping others first and putting my firm, Erie Shores Computer Inc., and family second. Many of the achievements I accomplished while serving on these boards and committees had enhanced the lives of the African Americans and Hispanics in Lorain County but I knew that it would be a mistake to take public credit for these successes. I knew that many of the leaders in the black and Hispanic communities would somehow view my activities as being self-serving.

Example: In 1985, after threatening to file a lawsuit against the Lorain County Commissioners for unlawful bid practices, my firm, Erie Shores Computer Inc., was awarded a $115,000 settlement. I donated computers, printers, software, and supplies to the Ministerial Alliance (an Alliance of Black ministers), valued at $15,000. A few days later, on a Saturday morning, while relaxing in my bathroom and scanning the *Chronicle* newspaper, there was my picture on the front page of the local section. It wasn't even a good picture of me. The article's heading read: "Jones has ulterior motive for donation to Lorain County Ministerial Alliance." This hit me like a ton of bricks in the chest. This article painted a picture of a perception that many in the black community had of me.

I could hardly wait until Monday morning to call Art Hudnutt, the owner of the *Chronicle Telegram* newspaper. Art and I knew each other quite well and had established a level of mutual trust, so when I called to schedule a meeting, he immediately scheduled it for the following day.

After exchanging niceties for a couple of minutes, I informed him that I was there to discuss the article published about me in his Saturday paper. After I ranted for probably five minutes, Art kept his cool and proceeded to informed me that the paper was not responsible for any of the information in the article about me. He informed me that the information in the article was provided by George Hodge, the vice president of the Elyria NAACP, and all his paper did was run the story that had come from another up-standing leader in the black community.

The information Art had provided left me speechless, as he knew it would. There was nothing I could say at the time that would make any sense or sound logical, so I sat there in Art's office in silence. After Art silenced me with his information, he decided that it was his opportunity to have me answer a couple of questions that had been puzzling him.

Art's first question was: "Jones, why is it, when blacks, such as your-self, do something to help the black community, they are attacked and viewed as negative by many in the black community?"

His second question was regarding black churches: "Larry, why are there so many black churches in Elyria?" His question put me deeper into a defensive posture because I had wondered the same thing upon arriving in Elyria. He then explained why he was con-cerned about so many churches. He went on to explain that in an average week, the Chronicle Telegram would receive five to seven requests for donations from these churches. Then he added, "And Larry, many of these churches have less than twenty members!"

I did not even attempt to answer his questions—questions for which I was pretty sure he already knew the answers. I walked away from that meeting feeling beaten and embarrassed because Art had made it clear that he knew why there were so many black churches in Elyria; and if he knew, then the majority of other whites knew.

When I asked my ninety-one-year-old friend, Ike Chapman, why were there so many black churches in Elyria, he shared the answer. Mr. Chapman stated that there were a couple of reasons for this: (1) African Americans found it very difficult to work together in harmony over a period of time, and (2) when the leadership of the churches had disagreements, instead of meeting and resolving the issues, one of the factions would leave and start a new church. I knew Art had seen this happen in Elyria many times over the years.

This meeting made it clear to me that no matter how much African Americans called each other brothers and sisters, the whites in power—and many others—knew that there was a wide span of jealously, mistrust, and fear within the African American communities. Overlooking these traits in two African American medical doctors, an African American attorney, and a business partner a few years later would lead to the destruction of my family's personal wealth and the financial stability of my business.

For fourteen years, from 1984 through the year 1998, Erie Shores Computer did business with white businesspeople, sometimes with just a handshake, and not one time did these businesspeople attempt to destroy me or my company. A few of them may have cheated Erie Shores out of two or three thousand dollars.

I had searched for African American tech firms that I could partner with between 1989 and 1997, but I was unsuccessful. Not until 1999 did I see an opportunity to work with, what I perceived as, a legitimate African American owned and operated company. The business was in the beverage industry. I felt great to have the opportunity to partner with a firm owned by other African Americans. This would prove to be the biggest mistake I would ever make as a businessman. Many of the African Americans who owned firms practiced the following philosophy: "If I am in business with you, for my business to be successful, your firm has to fail." There was little to no understanding from these businessmen of the proven fact that success will only come when both firms are successful financially.

CHAPTER TWENTY ONE

When the time came for me to leave the mill for US Steel's regional sales office in downtown Cleveland, Don Pass invited Barbara and me to dinner. Don was never married, and his mother lived with him most of the time—other than when he stayed overnight in the trailer that was parked on the US Steel property.

Don's mother joined us for dinner. Don ruled the mill with an iron fist, and to see the softer side of Don and how he treated his mother was quite revealing. Don wanted me to become a salesman for the mill and not accept the position in the district sales office. I thanked him but turned his offer down. I had not let anyone other than Barbara know how much I looked forward to leaving the mill.

I lost all contact with Don Pass after leaving US Steel, Lorain Works. I had heard about the passing of his mother, and Barbara and I knew that her passing would leave a big void in his life; and it did. Some years later, Don left US Steel and was later found dead on the streets of New York City. His appearance suggested that he had become a street person at the time of his death.

━┼ ┼━

I was now the first African American to hold the title of outside sales engineer for US Steel Corporation. The district sales office was in Cleveland, Ohio, on the thirty-third floor of the 100 Erieview Plaza Building.

I arrived at the office early that morning, and only a few employees had arrived. The first person I met was a young female in her mid-twenties. I introduced myself, and she welcomed me. From that welcome, it was clear to me that each of the seventy-five to one hundred office employees knew that I was coming. The young lady also knew that I had spent some time with the Dallas Cowboys. Then, not realizing what her actions were saying, she removed the sports section of her newspaper and shared it with me. What an experience I was in for, and what an education the district sales office employees would receive during my six-year office stay.

Everyone took turns introducing themselves to me, and afterward I was provided a desk in the sales area of the office. My immediate supervisor was Jack Gallander. I could tell that Jack had not been in the presence of—and definitely had not supervised by—an African American prior to this. I was quite comfortable in the office with an all-white cast. After all, I had experienced whites as the majority all of my life. Having lived in both worlds had served me well and had put me in a unique position in this office.

Jack introduced me to my inside sales representative and support staff. For the first three to four weeks I rode with the salesman who had managed the territory that I would be assuming. The sales visits went well, and afterward, I was presented my vehicle.

A company car, an attractive benefit plan, and a good salary made me feel like I had arrived at a great starting point in my new career.

Mike, the other African American who trained with me in Pittsburgh, did not receive an outside sales position, and I understood that he soon departed US Steel for another steel firm. With the $250,000 worth of sales training he had received from US Steel, I was quite sure that Mike would not have any problems finding quality employment. I have often wondered: if Mike had been as light-skinned as I, would he have been awarded this outside sales position instead of me?

CHAPTER TWENTY TWO

I had no idea that starting an Urban League chapter in Lorain County would be such a life-changing decision for me and my family. First of all, it thrust my family and me into the spotlight in Lorain County, and because of this spotlight, I would experience the good, the bad, and the ugly.

It was never my intention to become the leader of such a powerful organization as the Urban League of Lorain County, the affiliate of a powerful national organization. Because of this immediate and very visible notoriety, I became the interest of the black leadership, the political leadership, and the civic and business leadership, all for different reasons.

The black leaders in the cities and county were first fearful of me because so much power had been thrust upon me. They didn't know me very well, but it became clear to them that I was now in a position of power in the county, which no other black had possessed. This initial fear quickly evolved into fear, jealously, and envy.

There were no mainstream black businesses in the county in 1979; therefore, all of these factions viewed my position with US Steel as a powerful gateway between black and Hispanic communities and the business community. The black and Hispanic leaders only communicated with me when they needed something from the business or civic community that they could not achieve without my assistance. The white community and the businesses and civic organizations came to rely on me to guide them through hurdles and problems in the black and Hispanic/Latino communities. Before my presence on the various boards and committees, the liberal whites serving on those boards and committees were the voices for these minority communities. Because of this lack of minority participation on these boards, I began to suggest and recommend various African American and Hispanic/Latinos to various committees and boards that had never had representation. I had only one request of the boards or committee representatives: that they would not mention my name in any way when recruiting these individuals.

The political community was a different animal. There were a number of African American city council members in the three cities. (I will focus my comments on the blacks who represented the city of Elyria.) There were no black countywide office holders, and there had never been a black county-wide elected official. I attempted to stay as far away as I could from the political environment in Lorain County and city of Elyria, but as chairman of the Lorain County Urban League, staying nonpolitical was impossible.

Please understand; I was presiding as chairman of the league, and at the same time I was the first African American to become an outside sales engineer in the history of the US Steel Corporation. My sales territory for US Steel encompassed the territory from the west side of the Cleveland Flats to East 220th Street and south to the Independence city line. I mention this to you because, for many years, I held two full-time jobs: my paid position with US Steel and as chairman of the Urban League of Lorain County.

When I accepted the chairmanship of the league, there were three African Americans who had served on the Elyria city council for many years. Oberlin was the most liberal of the cities in Lorain County, but there was very little black leadership in the city, so the liberal whites made most of the decisions for the black community.

The city of Elyria was a different story when it came to blacks making decisions—or so it appeared. I am sure that there were many accomplishments in the black community that could be attributed to the three black city council members. A closer study revealed the true story of how these black leaders made decisions or at least agreed to decisions that affected the black community. There was a strong Democratic leadership in the county and city governments. The black council members owed—or at least thought they owed—their present and future success to the Democratic and union leadership in the county; therefore, they supported the wishes of these two organizations first, and then they supported the needs of the black community. In addition, whenever there was a benefit for the black community, the family members of these black politicians were the first, and most of the time the only ones, to benefit from their positions. At most, one of these black leaders would receive a secretarial or street sanitation position for a family member as restitution for their efforts. These political leaders demanded nothing; therefore, they received very little for their community, and in turn, their community demanded very little from their political leaders.

Permit me to share the meeting that took place on that infamous Sunday afternoon in the building at Midway Mall that presently houses Denny's Restaurant. It was during an off election year, and the most important political position to be filled in the city of Elyria was judge for the Elyria Municipal Court.

Ernie Roberts approached me and requested my support in getting a gentleman named George Ferguson elected to this judge seat. The biggest hurdle for George was to win the Democratic primary because he was not the pick of the county and city Democratic machine.

Ernie and I were both business owners, and after he provided background information on George Ferguson, I agreed to co-chair George's campaign committee with Ernie. George won the primary—over the wishes of the Democratic party—and was elected judge in the general election.

Prior to the general election, George asked me what I expected him to do for me if he won, and I told him that I wanted him to appoint the first African American in the history of the county to serve as bailiff in his court. George agreed and asked me to provide him some names of qualified persons. I already knew the person whom I would recommend to fill this bailiff position: a young man named Gary Dickerson.

Approximately two weeks after George's win, I was summoned to a Sunday meeting by Victor Stewart, chairman of the Lorain County Democratic party and Thomas Smith, chairman of the city of Elyria Democratic party. Upon my arrival, I was shocked to see all three of the black Elyria city councilmen (Bullocks, Jones, and Shores) and James Mitchell (a black community leader) at this meeting. Little did I know that these African American leaders had requested this meeting so that their leaders, Mr. Stewart and Mr. Smith, could alert me that these black gentlemen were the leaders in the black community. If I had not been so amused at this spectacle, I probably would have been extremely angry at these leaders, who felt that they needed these white men to speak for them.

It appeared that two of the councilmen had been promised a position by Stewart and Smith but realized that Stewart and Smith were no longer in control of awarding positions for Judge Ferguson; I now held that power. After a forty-minute meeting, everyone present realized that I had no plans to give up my power to have Judge Ferguson appoint my person as bailiff.

As soon as this meeting ended, I called Gary Dickerson and invited him and his parents over to my home that evening. I updated Gary about the meeting in which I had just participated. I told him that I was sure he would be contacted by Mr. Stewart, but there was nothing Mr. Stewart could do to prevent him from being named bailiff for Judge Ferguson. All he needed to do was to be quiet, listen, pay attention, and show respect when Vic Stewart summoned him.

Gary was summoned to a meeting in Vic Stewart's office that Monday afternoon. Present in the meeting were the same individuals who had been present in the Sunday meeting, excluding me. Stewart chastised Gary and stated in front of those present that he wanted to make sure that he, Gary, knew that these four black leaders were the leaders of the African American community and not Larry Jones, and that he should never forget that.

A few days later, I received a call from Judge Ferguson. He had what I thought was an excellent idea about the bailiff position. He suggested that I call Judge John Howard, the first African American judge in the history of Lorain County, and offer him the opportunity to hire Gray Dickerson as his bailiff. I suggested to George that it would be better if he approached Judge Howard. A couple of days later, Judge Ferguson informed me that he had suggested the idea to

Judge Howard, and he had immediately refused Ferguson's offer and had refused to have any additional discussions about the suggestion. Judge Ferguson, after Judge Howard's rejection, proceeded to hire Gary Dickerson as his bailiff.

We all know that politicians only carry out the wishes of the business leaders of the nation, state, county, and city; therefore, the political leaders of Lorain County and Elyria made very few decisions without directives from the business leaders. And I just happened to have at least two of the most powerful business, civic, county, and regional leaders on the Lorain County Urban League board. As chairman of the league, I was able to achieve major advances for the African American and Hispanic communities—achievements and advances that were intentionally never publicized.

In order to get to know the African American community better, I joined the NAACP chapter in Elyria, joined the Gentry Club (a social organization), and Barbara and I became well known by attending various social gatherings (given by the black, white, and Hispanic/Latino communities) throughout Lorain County.

CHAPTER TWENTY THREE

I grasped the outside sales job with US Steel, and most of my customers welcomed me without hesitation. It became very clear that being professional and performing services for the customer in a way that increased efficiency and saved the firm time and money cancelled out any racial prejudices that may have existed.

Within a few months on the job, I became a familiar and accepted entity in the sales office. I was well aware that I was representing not only myself but all African Americans because very few of the US Steel employees in that office had ever interacted on a social or professional level with African Americans—especially with a young African American male.

My biggest challenges came when attempting to work with my immediate supervisor, Jack Gallander. Jack was a manager who appeared to have achieved his position by kissing ass and sucking up to those in higher management positions; that included his immediate supervisor. The outside sales team under his supervision discounted his advice most of the time. Being new to the team, I attempted to work closely with Jack. After reaching a comfort level in my position, I would share my suggestions on how the sales teams could operate more efficiently. After my first few suggestions, I realized that Jack was presenting my suggestions to his supervisor, Scott Brinker, the district sales office manager, as his own and not giving me any credit. Jack appeared to have reached his "Peter principle" position with US Steel.

Jack's boss, Scott Brinker, appeared to be managing the district sales office because he enjoyed working for US Steel and not because he needed the money. He was a member of the Proctor and Gamble family. Scott had one weakness that everyone in the office knew about: he visited the downstairs lounge on a daily basis, where he drank his lunch most days.

One of my customers was located on the east side of the city of Cleveland—East 79th Street, to be exact. The owner was Frank, a "good ol' boy," who appeared to be around sixty-five years of age. During a two-year period, I had won his respect and trust by performing better than his former US Steel representative. Frank knew that I would do what was necessary to assure that his aircraft-quality steel was delivered on time and at the highest quality.

US Steel, as most other steel mills in the United States, was old and inefficient. One of my first responsibilities as a sales engineer was to visit the Port of Cleveland, with my binoculars, for the purpose of listing the foreign countries that were shipping steel into the United States. At that time a number of foreign countries were shipping steel, (dumping was the US definition) into the country at prices that were sixty to eighty dollars per ton lower than what it cost US mills to produce.

The US Steel mill that produced the aircraft-quality steel for Frank's firm had fallen behind in its production schedule due to a blast furnace problem. We had owed Frank three truckloads of steel for approximately two weeks, and one more week of delay would shut his plant down. Shutting his plant down would mean a delay in providing parts to his aircraft-industry customers.

I kept Jack, my manager, up to date on this critical situation, but I was leery of him accompanying me on any of my calls to Frank's firm. I guess Jack had decided that he needed to assist me with the problems we were causing Frank, so he informed me that he would be accompanying me on my customer calls that day. Knowing Jack as I had come to know him, I had a meeting with him and my inside sales representative, Gary, prior to leaving the office that morning. I alerted both Jack and Gary, again, about our status with Frank's steel delays, and that we were in serious trouble. I suggested how this delicate situation should be handled. I informed Gary that I would call him from Frank's office once Jack and I arrived, and that I would insist that he contact the mill again for status while I was on the phone. I had described Frank to Jack on numerous occasions and Gary had wondered how I had been able to get Frank to have such a high level of trust in me.

Jack and I arrived at Frank's firm, and the secretary announced us, and within five minutes Frank invited us into his office from the waiting room. I introduced Jack to Frank, and then I immediately began providing Frank an update on the blast furnace problem that was delaying his steel shipments. I had strongly suggested to Jack that he permit me to lead the discussions with Frank and that he listen closely to the conversation. Frank asked, "Jones, when can I expect my damn steel to be delivered?" I immediately asked Frank if I could use his phone to call my inside guy to get a real-time update because he had been in touch with the mill while we were on our way to his office.

My phone conversation with Gary relieved some of the tension because he was able to inform me that one load of Frank's steel would be arriving that next day—enough steel to keep Frank's machines operating. Frank was pleased to hear the news and I also informed him that his additional loads would arrive within three days.

Boy, I felt great because we had satisfied an important customer. What happened next was just pure stupidity on Jack's part. From out of nowhere, Jack commented, "Frank, do you have any orders to place with us today?" Frank looked at me and then at Jack and turned red faced and stated to Jack in a loud voice; "I have been waiting three weeks for you to ship my damn steel, and now you sit there and ask me for additional orders. Get the hell out of my office." When Jack and I stood to leave his office, Frank stated, "Jones, I want you to stay," and I continued to stand, not sitting again until Jack left the office. Once Jack was in the waiting room, Frank told me never to bring Jack back to his office again and proceeded to kept me in his office for approximately fifteen minutes, just to keep Jack waiting in the lobby.

Once Jack and I were in the car, I stated to Jack that I had warned him about Frank's personality. Jack was pissed because Frank had ordered him out of his office. I attempted to explain to Jack that he was wrong when he asked for additional orders, when we had not shipped the customer's present orders. Jack somehow felt that once he had been ordered out of the office, I should have accompanied him, no matter what Frank had requested, and Jack stated that I should not treat him that way again. East 79th Street was where Frank's firm was located, and the population of the area was 99 percent African American—the type of community where most of the dirty and polluted industries were housed.

By this time I was angry and stopped the car and told Jack that if he continued to talk that stupid shit to me, I would put him out of the car, and he would have to walk back to the office. Jack immediately ceased talking, and we never discussed that sales call again, nor did Jack ever visit or speak to Frank while I was the salesman for the account. Jack and I got along quite well after this sales call, and I attribute this to Jack being appreciative that I did what was necessary to keep an important customer. I also think he was appreciative that I kept my silence about what happened that day.

CHAPTER TWENTY FOUR

J ack's management style was a problem that I was able to work around, but there were more damaging and stressful situations that I would be forced to deal with. These problems involved the African American women who had been employed in these corporations as receptionists and or secretaries during the mid-1970s and 1980s. If I had only rarely experienced these problems with African American women in these corporations, I would not be sharing my experiences at this time.

The mid-1970s were the first years that African Americans had the opportunity to gain employment in large businesses and major corporations. Probably 85 to 90 percent of the African American and Hispanic/Latinos hired were hired in personnel or public relations positions in these firms.

As we all know, after the riots of the late 1960s and early 1970s, corporations opened a small door to hiring employees of the minority population. In order for these corporations to achieve the most visible successes and changes to their hiring practices, they proceeded to hire light-skinned African American, Hispanic, and Latino women in large numbers and omitted the hiring of African American and Hispanic/Latino males and dark-skinned women.

The reason for this hiring practice was simple to understand: when one minority woman was hired, two employment requirements had been fulfilled—a minority and a female. The dark-skinned women would continue to be discriminated against by whites and many of their light-skinned African Americans and Hispanic sisters. There was no interest by these corporations in hiring African American or Hispanic males.

I could only hope that these light-skinned African American, Hispanic, and Latino women understood why they were hired into the corporate workforce, while their dark-skinned sisters and African American, Hispanic, and Latino brothers were pretty much locked out of corporate America. Unfortunately, instead of working to assist their dark-skinned sisters and their male counterparts to gain entry into corporate America, many of these women worked to keep them out of corporate America—intentionally and unintentionally.

I was blessed to be one of the few African American males who was employed by corporate America during the mid-1970s. I know for a fact that in addition to my level of intelligence, my light skin color played an important role in my hiring.

I would come to know firsthand about the negative attitude and actions of many of the African American and Hispanic women after they were employed by these corporations. Many of my clients had hired black women as secretaries and receptionists, and these women were normally the first people I would see when calling on my customers. One would think that I would receive a pleasant and warm welcome or at least a professional welcome, just as my white counterparts received.

I well remember my first visit to a customer where an African American female had replaced the white female as the receptionist/ secretary. This young lady treated me as though I was not supposed to be there. She extended me no professionalism and very little respect. The level of disrespect was depressing, and at the same time, it pissed me off. Her attitude toward the white males who entered the room after I had arrived was professional and courteous. This attitude pretty much became the norm for me in most of the offices where I had to communicate with African American women to obtain an audience with the person I was there to see. It was as though many of these women had taken the role of "the doorkeeper." It appeared they felt they were there to keep other persons of color from getting in instead of assisting them to enter. My most difficult projects were creating action plans on how to best approach and appease these women, in order to get to see the person with whom I had the appointment.

Another experience I had on a regular basis happened whenever I entertained my customers at a restaurant for lunch or dinner. Seldom would the waiter or waitress assumed that I would be the one paying the tab. The observant ones would not assume but would place the check in the middle of the table if they were not sure who was paying the tab. But seldom was the invoice placed in the middle of the table; normally it was given to one of my white customers. Whenever that occurred, not only was the server embarrassed but my clients were also embarrassed. Quite a few times the server would pay a price for his or her actions by the size of his or her tip. Of course, I would avoid entertaining my customers at those restaurants as much as possible. I was well aware of the nasty things that could be performed on food between the kitchen and the table if I were too harsh in my criticisms.

After completing my first year as an outside sales engineer, I ranked in the top ten percentile of salespersons in the corporation.

In 1978, the steel industry was approximately fifteen months from a major recession. I was made aware of this fact by Dave, the senior purchasing agent at TRW, one of my customers. Dave, an economist, had shared many of his thoughts with me and strongly suggested that I should look for employment outside of the steel industry very soon. Within a few months the steel firms in the United States, including US Steel, began cutting management and inside sales jobs. Those who remained employed saw their salaries frozen and benefits cut. It was amazing how rapidly the steel industry was eroding. Just twelve months earlier, the union leadership at the Lorain Works had been pressing for US Steel to finance a health/exercise facility close to the mill for its members.

When the cuts came, they came sudden and hard. Although I was quite concerned, my job was secure for the present because very few outside sales positions were eliminated.

CHAPTER TWENTY FIVE

DAMN YOU AGAIN, WILLIE LYNCH

The Willie Lynch Letter: the Making of a Slave is the study of slave making. It described the rationale and the results of whites' ideas and methods for insuring the master/slave relationship.

Working in Cleveland and chairing the Lorain County Urban League was extremely stressful. The African American leaders in Lorain County continued to be afraid of the league and its leadership, even though some of those members were on the league's board. These individuals gave the impression that they were supportive of the league's program, but in private, they pushed a negative agenda against the league and its programs—programs that were focused on helping the African American and Hispanic/Latino communities. This sabotage from within went on for the first seven to eight years, until some of these leaders lost some of their power and connections.

The ironic fact was that the league's programs that were in place to assist the African American and Hispanic/Latino communities had received average success and were supported strongly by the business and civic communities but received little support from the Hispanic and African American leaders. During these seven years, the business and civic leaders became well aware of just how divided the African American and Hispanic/Latino leaders and communities really were. They had seen through the phony veil of closeness that was displayed in these communities. The NAACP chapters and EL Centro were the organizations that led in opposing the league's programs.

The league did its best to work with the various agencies with a similar focus, but very little progress was made. Because of the financial support from the business and civic communities, the league was able to survive and continue its programs in spite of the opposition.

My position with US Steel Corporation afforded me opportunities to be in the presence of powerful people throughout Northern Ohio. After attending a couple of meetings sponsored by the Greater Cleveland Growth Association, I was asked by James Wade, director of the Minority Input Committee, to serve as a member of the Input Committee's board. This committee had been formed to act as a liaison between the major businesses and corporations and the small businesses that were owned by African Americans, Hispanics/Latinos, and women. This committee would become the catalyst for me to eventuality start my technology firm in 1983.

Serving on this committee afforded me regular opportunities to meet and get to know many of the presidents and vice presidents of major corporations, large and small business owners, politicians, and civic leaders throughout Northern Ohio. Many of these leaders made it a point to invite me to their businesses for a tour, and I took advantage of a number of their invitations: Sherwin Williams, Eaton, Alcoa, Ohio Bell, and TRW Valve, just to name a few.

I had already experienced the sweet taste of business success when I had succeeded in turning the Lincoln University bookstore into a profitable venture. By interacting with these powerful people, I was sure that my knowledge of business would expand greatly; and it did.

CHAPTER TWENTY SIX

I t was now 1980, and I had not received a salary increase since arriving at the district sales office. This would have been okay if I had
not become aware that my manager had awarded raises to three of
his other outside sales engineers. My sales numbers were at the top of
the office sales chart and far beyond the three salespeople who had
received raises.

I approached Jack and stated that I felt I deserved a raise, and
that I was aware of the raises he had awarded his three other sales
reps. My visit caught Jack by surprise, and all he could say was that
he would have to discuss the matter with Mr. Brinker. I waited for
two days to hear form Jack, but Jack avoided me at every turn. Upon
arriving in the office a couple of days later, I called Mr. Brinker and
requested—and received—a meeting later that afternoon.

I explained my situation and concerns to Scott, and he understood my concerns and promised me that he would review my status.
A few days later Scott called me to his office to inform me that he had
submitted my concerns to US Steel headquarters in Pittsburgh. Scott

also informed me that there was a possibility I would be invited to become a part of the US Steel office in upper New York State. I knew I would refuse to accept this move due to the more severe weather in Buffalo; Cleveland weather was harsh enough.

For approximately four months prior to approaching Jack about the salary increase, I had been in negations to accept the regional sales manager position with a minority-owned steel service center, headquartered in Detroit, Michigan. One of the service center owners was Dave Bing. Dave had recently retired from the National Basketball League and was now part owner of a steel warehousing firm: Bing Steel. Oliver Isaac was the other part owner of Bing Steel. My salary issue at US Steel was only one of the reasons I decided to accept the regional sales manager position with this steel warehousing firm. Immediately after deciding to depart US Steel, I put my notice in writing to Jack and Scott. My decision caught both by surprise. Neither one approached me that day. I would learn later that Scott had alerted headquarters about my decision to leave US Steel.

The next morning Scott asked to meet with me. We discussed why I had made a decision to leave the firm. Scott and Jack were pretty sure that I was upset with their treatment of me, and that once I was no longer employed by the firm, I would file a lawsuit. I had made no comments in our prior meetings that would have led them to believe that a lawsuit was pending.

I had returned to my desk for only a couple of hours when Scott called to inform me that Rube Perrin, a vice president of U S Steel was on the line and wanted to speak with me. I had met Rube during my Pittsburgh training session; he was a Yale graduate who was on a fast track with the company.

Rube informed me that he had received a copy of my resignation letter and wanted to discuss it with me. Our meeting needed to be face to face, and to achieve this he would send the US Steel jet to Burke Lakefront Airport in downtown Cleveland to fly me to Pittsburgh, if I agreed. Burke Lakefront Airport was a very short distance from the building that housed the Cleveland district sales offices.

I agreed to take that flight to Pittsburgh and meet with Rube. The next day, I boarded the US Steel jet and flew to Pittsburgh and had a dinner meeting with Rube at his beautiful and spacious hilltop home. Rube did not hesitate with his remarks. He offered me a 50 percent pay increase if I would remain with US Steel. I had made up my mind to leave the company and had already accepted the regional sales position with American Basic Industries, the steel service center.

I shared my status with Rube and then assured him that I would not be taking any legal action against US Steel. Rube then admitted that this was a real relief to hear. He then shared with me some of his immediate plans, including his intention to leave US Steel soon for a position with a Wall Street firm. After our three-hour visit, I thanked Rube for the invitation, and Rube thanked me for coming. I was then driven back to the airport and flown back to Cleveland. I am sure that Jack and Scott were relieved when Rube updated them about our dinner meeting.

CHAPTER TWENTY SEVEN

Prior to releasing my US Steel vehicle, I drove it to Detroit to pick up my Bing Steel vehicle. I was ready to begin my new career. I had had my fill of corporate America, a place where independent thinking was a negative and where one could easily get lost in the company's levels of bureaucracy. I viewed this new firm as being small enough where I could make a difference and become successful.

A few days prior to reporting to the Detroit location of Bing Steel, Oliver called to informed me that he and Dave had decided to go their separate ways, and that I would be going with him and his firm, American Basic Industries, to Michigan City, Indiana. This information hit me like a ton of bricks. Had I made the biggest mistake in my early life by leaving US Steel and accepting a position with an unknown black-owned steel warehouse? No matter what, it was now too late to undo the life-changing moves I had just made.

Things would only get worse. During my first meeting with Oliver as an employee of American Basic Industries, I learned that the monthly salary I had been promised, in writing, would now become monthly draws. Anyone who knows the history of Michigan City, Indiana, knows that it is one of the cities in the Chicago area that was used as a haven for the mafia during the period from the early 1900s through the 1970s.

Instead of assuming the management of a regional sales territory, I was now the salesperson who was expected to develop and support this new territory. Nothing was as it had been promised to me. The contract I had signed wasn't worth the paper used for the contract. I thought about suing but became aware American Basic Industries had very few assets. Later I would be pleased I had not taken legal actions against the firm.

I did a lot of additional praying during those first few weeks. I already knew American Basic Industries would only be a brief part of my employment future. I also knew that I had no choice but to continue with this firm and receive the monthly draws—draws that were approximately 60 percent of my US Steel salary; and of course, I now had no expense account or benefits.

My office was in my home, so I decided that my territory would become the same as when I was employed by US Steel. I knew that this was going to be an extremely difficult task—attempting to develop a successful steel clientele just when the bottom was falling out of the steel industry—but I had no other options.

⚊⭰ ⭲⚊

Prior to leaving US Steel, I had made excellent use of my contacts at the Greater Cleveland Growth Association. I had received an education on business development and management. Most importantly, I had contacts at the Growth Association and at numerous firms that were eager to assist me in whatever I requested. I knew it was critical that I stayed in touch with these individuals and what better way than continuing to be an active and very visible member of the Growth's Minority Input Committee.

By now I had the close attention of Eric Nord, chairman and CEO of Nordson Corporation and Scribner L. Fauver, partner in the law firm of Fauver, Tattersal & Gallagher. These two powerful Republicans had served on the first Urban League's board and were well aware of my management skills and abilities. I now had their attention whenever I needed it.

Eric and Scrib were extremely concerned about the lack of equality and representation of the African American and Hispanic/Latino communities when compared to the white communities in Lorain County. It could be said that there was a very high wall at the Lorain County, Cuyahoga County lines, and this wall had caused Lorain County's advancements to lag thirty to forty years behind the times. Serving as the chairman of the Urban League for twelve years gave me a clear and in-depth understanding of Lorain County. This is why I began calling the county "Slorain County."

Eric Nord, a few other leaders in the minority community, and I were keenly aware of the discrimination and major race-related problems in Lorain County. Eric and Scrib had known about these problems for many years but had no vehicle to use to change the status quo; that is, not until the Urban League was established. Eric and Scrib, both white and Republican, were very intelligent and knew that they could not be the visible ones to lead the push for these social and economic changes.

I will forever remember two comments that Eric Nord made during one of my many meetings with him. Washington Avenue was where many of Elyria's wealthiest families lived. At some point, the

Elyria decision makers, in their infinite wisdom, decided to build the city's YMCA facilities on Washington Avenue.

Eric lived in Oberlin and was very sincere when he stated to me, "Larry, why would the decision makers in Elyria build their YMCA facilities on the wealthiest street in the city?" He already knew the answer to his question. Eric was also very disappointed with the decision making of the Lorain County officials and many of the city of Lorain officials. Eric stated that what compelled him to build his Nordson Corporation's world headquarters in Cuyahoga County, less than a half mile from the Lorain County line, was due to the backward thinking of the Lorain County leaders and decision makers.

⚒⚒

My leadership and visibility while these changes were taking place in Lorain County thrust me into an even more attractive position from the perspective of the county's business and civic leaders.

I well remember that day in 1982 when, as regional sales manager of American Basic Industries, I made a sales call on a firm in Elyria. This was a well-run firm that kept abreast of any new technology that would advance the firm. When I arrived, I was greeted by and spent most of my time talking with the firm's executive assistant. During the conversation, I noticed what appeared to be a computer (IBM PC) with a plant placed on top of it. I posed the question, "Why is there a plant on top of the computer?" The young lady stated, "The owner purchased this thing in Cleveland, and no one here knows how to operate it."

This young lady had no idea the importance and power of the comment that she had just shared with me. Her comment started me on my journey into the strange field of computers.

I knew little to nothing about computers, but I knew that if one of the most progressive firms in Lorain County had purchased a computer and was using it as a flower holder, there was a technology void in Lorain County. After a brief amount of investigating, I realized there was only one computer firm in the county, and it carried Atari products and no business-type computers. The void was in the computer hardware, software, and training areas, and I knew that I had to find a way to fill this void, while at the same time performing enough work for American Basic Industries to earn the draw that I was receiving.

After approximately nine months, my American Basic activities became secondary to my focus on starting my own company. By early 1983, I was sure that I would incorporate at some time during that year. I researched and gathered large amounts of information and felt pretty comfortable about striking out on my own. That was a good feeling because American Basic Industries was experiencing financial difficulties. I was sure that these financial difficulties were much worse that Oliver had led me to believe, so I sped up the process of starting my technology firm.

I had always thought that Oliver had a person or persons from whom he had to seek approval prior to major financial decisions being made for American Basic. My thoughts were later confirmed when I was invited to Las Vegas to meet with a person whom he called a business associate. The plane landed in Vegas, and I was driven approximately thirty minutes out into the desert. As we pulled up to this mansion-looking home, I immediately became somewhat nervous because I had not been given any specifics about this meeting.

Oliver greeted me and welcomed me to the house. We talked about my trip and other unimportant things for an hour or so. Oliver had informed me that he had a home in the Bahamas and had invited Barbara and me to use it on vacation. I had wondered, at times, how Oliver could afford a home in the Bahamas. I retired to my room where I would spend the night because the person whom I was there to meet had not yet arrived. I was informed that I would be notified upon his arrival, and the meeting would take place.

Around eleven o'clock that evening, there was a knock on my door, informing me that the gentleman had arrived and was ready to meet with me. I walked into the room and saw this white, Jewish gentleman sitting at the other end of what appeared to be a long dining-room table. Oliver was seated in the chair to his left. He instructed me to sit at the other end of the table, which put me in the position directly facing him.

No one had to tell me who was in charge in the room. Now I was feeling quite nervous, and when this gentleman began to talk, I knew that I did not want to be there. It appeared that Oliver had suggested that I would be a good candidate for a higher position in the firm. I was remembering an old saying as I sat there: "If you don't know the rules of the game, don't play in it."

After about fifteen to twenty minutes of questions and answers, this gentleman stared at me in amazement, and I knew why. My responses to his numerous questions had made it appear that I was a little off in the head. The meeting lasted for approximately twenty-five minutes and ended without the niceties present at its beginning. My introduction to Oliver's business associate did not include his last name.

That was the first and last time that I would see this gentleman. The next morning, upon meeting Oliver, I could tell that he was not pleased. I knew I had disappointed him with my interview. He did not offer me any breakfast, and the chauffer returned me to the airport approximately three hours prior to my scheduled departure.

As I sat there in the Vegas airport, I felt a great relief just knowing that I had intentionally given the worst job interview of my life. I knew that I did not want to play in the game being offered me because I was sure it would be a game that I would be expected to possibly play in for the remainder of my life.

A couple of months after this meeting I decided to submit my letter of resignation to Oliver. I thanked him for the opportunity to work for American Basic Industries. I felt good because I knew that I had just dodged a bullet. Oliver and I never discussed or mentioned that meeting in the desert of Vegas.

CHAPTER TWENTY EIGHT

With the guidance of Attorney Fauver, I incorporated Erie Shores Computer in June 1983.

I knew how to start a company because of the seminars provided by the Cleveland Growth Association. Now all I needed was capital to start my firm. Business owners and corporate managers were ready to provide advice, but I knew that financial assistance would be a different story.

Once again my contacts through the Urban League would prove to be of great value.

I remembered what Eric Nord had stated to me three years prior: "Larry, if I can assist you in any way, just let me know." This was now the time to request Eric's assistance. I arranged a meeting with Eric, and he brought along his friends: Attorneys Scribner Fauver and William Ginn. Mr. Ginn was the managing partner in the law firm of Thompson, Hine, and Flory. I made my presentation to these gentlemen and provided a draft of my new firm (Erie Shores Computer Inc.) along with a proposed budget for the first two years. Within a week, Eric informed me that he, his brother Evan, and William Ginn had decided to invest $15,000 each in Erie Shores Computer. My funding prayers had been answered.

Now all I needed was someone who knew something about computers. The league had hired Raymond Little, an African American to install its multiuser system. I made an assumption that Ray would probably be interested in becoming a part of my new computer firm. Ray had recently left the employment of IBM at the time of our meeting. His stay with the technology giant was over—for reasons I would become aware of less than twelve months later. Ray did not know a great deal about computers, but he knew more than anyone else, so that made him an expert in Lorain County. It did not take a lot of convincing for Ray to come on board with me, especially knowing that I had agreed to finance the company.

One thing I was sure of was that I would build a firm that was diverse in its employees, and through the league, I would continue to be vocal about the lack of equality and business opportunities for African American, Hispanics, and Latinos in Lorain County. I had no idea at that time that my visible focus on the advancement of minorities in Lorain County would make me a target of a few powerful politicians and, later, the Lorain County prosecutor. What would prove to be extremely depressing for me was the fact that the leaders in the African American, Hispanic, and Latino communities, whom I had worked with tirelessly in the pursuit of equality, would end up not supporting me and my family when the devastating attacks came.

The name Erie Shores Computer Inc. came because Lorain County was located on the banks of Lake Erie. Erie Shores' first office space was located on the third floor of the old Robinson Building at the corner of Broad and Washington Avenue, in downtown Elyria.

The office was two small rooms, small enough where one telephone with a long cord could service the entire office.

I had met a young lady, Patricia Sims, through her employment at the league. I felt that Patricia could serve as a good secretary for Erie Shores Computer, and she had assisted Little while he installed the league's office computer system.

Pat began as the secretary for Erie Shores and rose within the company to the position of vice president and earned ownership in the company. She was a dedicated employee who remained with Erie Shores for eighteen years, until its demise in 2003.

━━┥╀╊┝━━

I had planned for Erie Shores Computer Inc. to service the businesses in the county by providing sales, delivery, installation, training, and repair of IBM business computers and printers. In order to achieve this, I had to hire a computer technician and purchase a company van. While I was performing these tasks, Ray and Pat were buying office supplies and installing the office equipment.

The first three months were extremely slow. Only a few small local businesses used our services. I was pretty sure that once the business community heard about Erie Shores, they would be interested in supporting a local computer firm. After all, Erie Shores was the only firm in Lorain County that focused on providing computer and related services to the business community.

Erie Shores hired a technician and purchased a van, which made the firm legitimate and visible. More and more small businesses began to call for assistance. I began to see the limits of Ray's computer knowledge and knew the company would soon need to hire someone with more computer knowledge than he possessed.

I truly believe God blessed me with favor because out of nowhere, a young man named Richard Brown, who had just graduated from Dartmouth University, began to visit the Erie Shores office. Richard came by to use the computers, and soon he began to assist with phone calls, answering technical questions that no one else could answer. I observed Richard's actions and the ease with which he answered all technical questions that were posed in person and via phone. I knew that I had received spiritual favors.

At the same time, while being blessed with the presence of Richard, my troubles with Ray were beginning to surface. Because of my association with the Greater Cleveland Growth Association, I had gained knowledge about how to complete and submit sealed bids.

Erie Shores' first sealed bid opportunity came in the summer of 1984, approximately fourteen months after Erie Shores had opened its doors. This was a bid request for a large quantity of computers and printers for the city of Cleveland, Ohio. Erie Shores had received its Minority Business Certification a few months prior. This certification assured minority participation in city of Cleveland bids, up to 15 percent on most large bids.

I felt that Erie Shores was in a position to bid on this contract as the prime bidder because I had worked hard and had been successful in getting two insurance firms to provide Erie Shores bonding for bids up to one million dollars.

There was one very unusual question every bidder had to answer before bidding on a city of Cleveland contract. That question was related to whether the firm or I, personally had ever had any activity with or related to members of the Irish Republican Army (IRA). I thought this was a strange question for a governmental entity to ask of a bidder. The reason for this question would become clear to me around the year 2000 because of an incident in the Cuyahoga County Recorder's Office.

Erie Shores bid on the city of Cleveland computer requirement, and when the sealed bids were opened, Erie Shores' bid was the second best and lowest. We had come so close to winning our first major contract. I was dejected about coming so close but not winning, but this exercise had given me the know-how and energy to look forward to future bidding opportunities.

I called the office after the bid opening and gave Pat the news that we had placed second in the bid process. Pat immediately informed Ray, and when I returned to the office, Ray had departed and Pat was concerned about how his attitude had changed as soon as she had told him that Erie Shores had not won the bid. She informed me that Ray had informed her that he was resigning from Erie Shores. She had also noticed that Ray had removed something from the company computer prior to leaving the office. I had become somewhat concerned about Ray's attitude a couple of weeks prior to his resignation notice.

⇒∈⊹ ⊹∋⇐

The next night Ray arrived at the office to retrieve additional items and information off the Erie Shores office system. I had anticipated that Ray would possibly return to the office unannounced. Ray was shocked when he realized that I was in the office. I asked Ray what was going on, and, if he had resigned, why was he at the office? Ray stated that he did not have to tell me anything and proceeded to attempt to log into the office computer. I asked him to remove himself from the office, but he continued to log into the system.

Ray stood approximately six feet, three inches tall and weighed around two hundred forty pounds. I was the same height and weighed approximately twenty pounds less, but my body was stronger. After my third time requesting Ray to leave the office, he jumped up from the chair that he was in, and as he turned, he found himself within two feet of me. Before Ray could finish his next statement of defiance, I pounded a left into his chest, which sent him sprawling to the floor. Before he could regain his senses, I had positioned myself on my knees behind him, with one arm around his neck and the other arm and hand coupling his chin. I could have easily snapped his neck with a full jerk of his head.

Ray was in a sitting position, still attempting to regain his senses, when a rage and fear like I had not experienced since the race riots of the late sixties, overwhelmed me. I realized that I had Ray's life literally in my hands at that moment. A few seconds later, while my arm remained around Ray's neck, I let Ray know that he was lucky I had decided not to snap his neck. I told him I was going to release him and instructed him to leave the office immediately—instructions he followed upon standing. Afterward, I would wonder what had kept me from breaking his neck.

I followed Ray from the third floor office to the street level. As I watched him leave, he headed south on Broad Street. I knew immediately where he was headed: to the police station located two blocks south.

I phoned Barbara and alerted her about what had just happened and told her that Ray had gone to the police station to file a complaint against me. Barbara, in her infinite wisdom, made this comment; "Larry, everyone knows you in Lorain County; how many know Ray'?" I knew I had to somehow resolve this potentially explosive negative situation.

I immediately walked to the police station and observed Ray completing his complaint. This was when I informed the officer in charge that I wanted to file a complaint. I knew that Ray was a little concerned when the officer greeted me by name. Most of the officers knew me because I had been involved in the police department's "civilian ride-along program." Ray completed his complaint, and so did I. Afterward, I went home, where Barbara continued to enlighten me about why my actions had been inappropriate.

Early the next morning I returned to the office and decided to call the police station for some guidance. I was informed that if Ray was going to pursue charges, he would be required to file those charges at the city prosecutor office, at City Hall. I was positive Ray would proceed with his charges against me, so I would need to speak with him prior to his reaching the prosecutor's office. The officer suggested that if I wanted to discuss this with Ray prior to him reaching the prosecutor's office, I should probably wait for him at City Hall.

When I arrived at City Hall, the building had not opened for business, so I was sure that Ray had not arrived. I did not have to wait long before Ray entered the door where I was standing. I really did not want to apologize to him because of the underhanded things he had done to the company, but I knew that an apology was necessary.

As Ray entered the door, I told him I wanted to apologize to him for my actions the night before. As I was apologizing, Ray continued to walk further into the building, and I came very close to bopping him in the back of the head; after all, he had attempted to remove critical data from the Erie Shores office computer. It was my second request to talk when he stopped to hear what I wanted to say. I proceeded to restate that I was sorry for my actions against him and wanted to resolved the matter without any legal actions. Ray was ready to listen to my offer.

I told Ray that I was willing to purchase his shares of ownership in Erie Shores, the shares that I had given him a little more than a year earlier. My purchase offer piqued Ray's interest because of his present financial condition. I told Ray I was willing to buy his shares for six hundred dollars. Approximately twenty-four hours later, Ray called and said he wanted $850.00 for his shares, and I agreed to pay him his asking price.

I immediately contacted my friend and attorney, Scribner L. Fauver, the attorney who would become the Erie Shores Computer corporate legal counsel and my family's personal counsel. Scrib told me that if I had agreed to pay the $850 to Ray, I should bring the check to his office, and he would have Ray come over and sign the documents necessary to sever his ownership in Erie Shores. The future of Erie Shores appeared quite dim at the time, but I had to stay focused to avoid becoming depressed.

The Erie Shores executive team now included Pat, Richard, and I. Months prior, I had made a promise to Richard. That promise was that if he continued to play a critical role in the Erie Shores operations, he would be awarded a 10 percent ownership in Erie Shores. I had become aware that probably no one else in Northern Ohio knew as much about computer hardware and software as Richard Brown. I knew the company could not afford Richard's worth; therefore, I gave him the freedom to set his own hours. He was elated at my offer to him and immediately accepted it.

CHAPTER TWENTY NINE

Approximately two weeks after the city of Cleveland computer sealed-bid opening, I received a call from the director of purchasing for the city of Cleveland. Director Bill Moon first needed to confirm that he was indeed speaking to the owner of Erie Shores Computer Inc. Once the confirmation was complete, Bill informed me that the firm that had submitted the lowest and best bid on the computer contract had been disqualified, and since Erie Shores Computer was the second lowest and best bidder, the computer contract was now being offered to Erie Shores Computer. I immediately agreed to accept and fulfill this computer contract.

I called Richard and Pat into my area of the office and informed them that we had been awarded the city of Cleveland computer contract. You can imagine the joy that filled the office that day.

Now all I had to do was to obtain the financing needed to fulfill this one-million-dollar contract. The Erie Shores corporate account had been established at Lorain National Bank (LNB). Lorain

National was truly a community bank. It was also a member of the Federal Government's Small Business Administration's Small Business Loan Program. Therefore, I was pretty sure there would be no problem in acquiring the financing needed to fulfill this city of Cleveland contract.

A few days after the contract was awarded to Erie Shores the Chronicle newspaper carried an article about the award. After becoming aware of the contract award to Erie Shores, Ray attempted to reestablish his prior ownership in the company. I immediately placed a call to Attorney Fauver. He assured me that he had received the necessary signed documents from Ray where it would be impossible for him to claim any ownership in Erie Shores Computer.

I called LNB and scheduled a meeting with the business loan department. Upon arriving at the bank's headquarters in downtown Lorain, I met with the business loan officer and shared with him the great news that Erie Shores had been awarded a computer contract by the city of Cleveland. I provided the loan officer a copy of the contract and answered the questions posed. The loan officer informed me that it would take a couple of days to make a decision because the loan committee would not meet until that next day.

Two days later the loan officer called and asked me to return to the downtown Lorain headquarters for a meeting. I arrived and, in a brief five-minute meeting, was informed that the bank had declined my request for a loan to finance the Erie Shores contract with the city of Cleveland. What really pissed me off was the bank's offer to provide me a car or home loan instead.

I had estimated that Erie Shores would need at minimum of one million dollars to finance this contract. My mother had taught me to believe that, where there is a will, there is a way. Again I prayed for guidance, knowing that LNB was the only bank at which Erie Shores had established a relationship. Later that afternoon I came to the conclusion that I would need the assistance of my friend, Eric Nord.

I knew this was again a good reason to call Eric for assistance. I also knew that he would be impressed by the fact that Erie Shores had been awarded such a large contract.

I called Eric and gave him the exciting news about being awarded the city of Cleveland contract. He congratulated me. I then informed him that the Erie Shores corporate account had been established at Lorain National Bank, and that I had met with the business loan officer at LNB to acquire financing for the contract, and that my request for a loan had been denied.

Eric's comment to me was, "Larry, let me make a phone call, and I will call you back within the hour." Within thirty minutes, I received Eric's return call. He instructed me to arrive at Lorain National's headquarters the next morning at 9:00 a.m. for a meeting with management.

I arrived at the bank around 8:30 a.m., and upon arriving, the secretary of the president, Mr. Stanley Pijor, greeted me and escorted me to Mr. Pijor's office, where I awaited his arrival. This was when I realized that I would be meeting with the president of Lorain National Bank. Mr. Pijor arrived and greeted me and invited me into the private section of his office. Stan and I got to know quite a lot about each other that morning. Our meeting lasted for approximately forty minutes, and only in the last five minutes did we discuss the financing of the computer contract. Stan informed me that Erie Shores Computer had been approved for an eight-hundred-thousand-dollar line of credit. His question was: Did I think this amount was enough to cover my needs? I told Stan, yes, and he then asked if I had any working capital, and I told him no, not really understanding the need for "working capital" at the time. Stan immediately arranged for Erie Shores to have $200,000 for working capital. I departed the bank on cloud nine. I not only had my financing, I had working capital because one of the most powerful men in the county had paved the way for Erie Shores. In obtaining this financing, I had met the president of one of the two largest banks in the county. As I reflect back on this process, sometimes I think that the loan process had been made too easy for me to understand the difficulty other minority businesses encountered when attempting to obtain financing. Stan would become a good business friend for many years.

Well, the city of Cleveland one-million-dollar contract turned out to be a one-million-five-hundred-thousand-dollar contract. Erie Shores made a very decent profit from this contract—enough profit to repay Lorain National its loan in full, one year in advance, and to buy back the $60,000 of Erie Shores Computer stock, which Eric and Evan Nord and William Ginn had purchased to assist in Erie Shores' startup. All three gentlemen refused to accept any interest or dividend on the repurchase of their stock.

⇒⟨⟩⇐

Erie Shores was in the beginning of its third year of operation and was already operating at a profit, and this profit run would continue for the next fifteen years.

Although headquartered in Lorain County, Erie Shores was not very successful obtaining business there. Only approximately 4 percent of the firm's sales were generated in Lorain County. Many times I had considered moving the Erie Shores headquarters from Lorain County, and I would have if I had not made a promise to the two gentlemen who had given so much of their time and money to the Urban

League of Lorain County and assistance to Erie Shores Computer. I had made a promise to Eric and Scrib that I would keep Erie Shores Computer headquartered in Lorain County. Eric and Scrib felt strongly that the success of Erie Shores—and my personal success— could be the catalyst needed for changing the business and social perception and attitude toward African Americans and Hispanics in the county. They felt strongly that a successful black-owned, mainstream firm, with an owner who was committed to helping the community, would greatly enhance the county.

Over a fifteen-year period, Erie Shores grew to employ up to thirty-eight people and expanded to five additional locations: Cleveland, Ohio; Columbus, Ohio; Lakeland, Florida; Dayton, Ohio; and Pittsburgh, Pennsylvania. Erie Shores' biggest and most profitable expansion was the Columbus expansion.

CHAPTER THIRTY

While working twelve to fifteen hours a day operating Erie Shores, I continued to serve as chairman of the Urban League's board of directors, in addition to serving on eight other critical boards. To guarantee the success of Erie Shores and knowing that I was short on assistance, I set up a portable bed in my office because I knew I would be working fourteen- to sixteen-hour days. This bed remained in my office for approximately three years.

I seldom spent time with my family, but I made sure that I represented the African American and Hispanic/Latino communities on the many critical boards in the county. I did not know how to "just say no." Many in the minority communities were afraid to serve on boards and committees with white people. Most would not admit their fear, but I heard all of their excuses, and the bottom line was fear of association. This fear of association led all of the boards and organizations that really wanted to have minority representation directly to me. I then identified those African Americans, Hispanics, and Latinos whom I felt were not afraid to represent. Only, if I had it to do all over again; I would not attempt to be everything to everyone because it is a recipe for disaster.

The most critical boards and committees on which I served during a twenty-year period were as follows;

1. Urban League of Lorain County (board chair)
2. United Way of Greater Lorain County (first African American)
3. Community Foundation of Greater Lorain County (first African American)
4. African American Fund (board chair)
5. Lorain County Board of Mental Health (first African American; board Chair)
6. Lorain County 20/20 Committee (first African American)
7. Lorain County Community Action Agency (board chair)
8. Greater Cleveland Growth Association (Minority Input Committee)
9. Premier Bank Board of Directors (first African American)
10. FirstMerit Bank Board of Directors (first African American)
11. Vice President, National Chapter, Friends of Amistad

When there was the need for minority representation and input, my phone rang, and I always said yes. Two of the boards were different from all the rest: the bank boards on which I served. These were the only two boards that paid a salary to serve.

I owe my first bank board membership to John Kriegbaum, who was then the president of Premier Bank and Trust. John was Jewish and made it one of his priorities for the bank to be enhanced by my input. I had proven to the community and the bank board members that I was well qualified to serve on a bank board. After all, I was the only African American who had owned and operated a successful mainstream firm in the county's history.

I was already a life member of the NAACP and member in good standing of the Urban League. In 1992, because of my association with the white business community, I was the first African American to be invited to become a member of the Elyria Rotary Club. I accepted and went on to become a Paul Harris Fellow. Through my participation in the Rotary Exchange Program, Barbara and I were host to a female high school exchange student from Germany for an entire school year.

⚓

I felt that I was being very productive in growing Erie Shores and the Urban League. In both entities, I made sure that there was diversity in employment. Erie Shores had the most diverse employee record of small firms in Lorain County. This achievement was pretty easy to maintain during the firm's sixteen most productive years of operation.

There were a number of setbacks during those years of growth; hiring and retaining good personnel were at the forefront. I worked hard to maintain diversity in the firm, but in doing so, my biggest problems were caused by the African American employees: not reporting to work, not reporting to work on time, subpar work, and theft were the major problems I encountered.

I also learned that to have an effectively run office in a small firm, one has to pay close attention to the dynamics and interactions between office staff, especially when working on group projects. The most serious office problems at Erie Shores occurred because of the decisions and actions of Anthony Mash, the Erie Shores Sales Manager. Anthony was Italian American, and he just assumed that he was superior to the other managers in the firm, so he took privileges that I should have put a stop to very early on. Too late, I would realize that Anthony didn't really care if the company made money, as long as he received his salary, sales commissions, and bonuses.

I will describe the most blatant visible actions by two of Erie Shores' employees: The first was when an employee was caught stealing computers by carrying them out the back door of the office building. This was an employee to whom I had advanced a loan earlier in the year so that he could pay personal bills. I realized then if Ed would steal from my firm, after providing him a substantial loan, he did not deserve to be employed by Erie Shores.

The second theft occurred while I was transacting business in Boca Raton Florida. Erie Shores had won a small contract with the city of Cleveland to supply thirty specially built high-powered computers to its water department. Instead of delivering these expensive systems to the city of Cleveland, the Erie Shores deliveryman, after loading the delivery truck, drove approximately two miles to one of the housing projects in Elyria. There, from the back of the truck, he sold these $3,500 systems for between fifty and seventy-five dollars each. Some of the systems were exchanged for crack.

Everyone who bought these systems or observed this Erie Shores employee's action, knew that a crime was being committed but did nothing to stop it or to report the crime. They knew that it was Erie Shores' equipment this person was selling because of the large letters on the truck. Instead of stopping this crime, they participated in it by purchasing systems. Less than one year earlier, Erie Shores had given out more that eighty Thanksgiving turkeys to families in that same housing development.

The Elyria police just happened by and observed the Erie Shores truck parked in a location where it should not have been parked.

They were only able to save four of these systems from being sold. When they arrested the driver, he was already high off crack that he had exchanged for a system. Hindsight told me that one of my biggest employee mistakes was not prosecuting those employees who deserved it.

The Erie Shores delivery man had used so much crack that he remained high for two days. Upon his release from jail, he had his lady friend visit Erie Shores and request his last paycheck. I will not share with you my comments to her, but she departed without the check that she had expected to receive.

During the next seven years, numerous persons shared with me the names of some of the citizens who had received some of those Erie Shores systems. I was dismayed to learn the names of four of those who had my systems. I visited the homes of a number of the city's upstanding citizens and observed my systems in their homes.

⇢⇠

Even though Erie Shores geared its sales to the business community, during its fifteen years of operations, more than two thousand white families purchased systems from Erie Shores, while only four African American families purchased computers from Erie Shores.

Two of the four black families that purchased their systems from Erie Shores Computer were asked to return their systems for a full refund due to the extra services that were being demanded. The process used by these families was to get a price from the Best Buy Store down the street and then come to Erie Shores for a better price. Erie Shores agreed to meet Best Buy's price and, in addition, included the following services: delivered system and printer to the home, set up equipment, and provided one hour of training. Best Buy offered these services for an additional cost. After all of these free extras, these two families wanted even more. This was when I decided to cut my losses and refunded the two families the full amount they had paid for the systems.

━━◈ ◈━━

CHAPTER THIRTY ONE

I have always believed that everyone deserves a second chance. That is one of the main reasons I hired Jessie, an ex-con from the Mansfield Correctional Institution, but sometimes providing second chances can be dangerous. I gave Jessie a position in the Dayton office, where he worked with John, a retired Air Force officer. John appeared to be color blind; therefore, I knew that he would represent Erie Shores well in the Dayton area as the purchasing agent for Erie Shores. This was the Erie Shores office responsible for fulfilling the company's thirty-eight-million-dollar Wright-Patterson Air Force Base computer contract.

Little did I know that this trust I had put in ex-con Jessie would be the beginning of the downfall of the Erie Shores Computer's Dayton operation. I only had the opportunity to visit the Dayton office once weekly, and in my absence, Jessie proceeded to intimidate John to the point that John resigned from the company. Jessie then decided he would drive the Erie Shores Computer van to Bronx, New York, to visit his relatives. Upon finding out about Jessie's actions, instead of filing charges against him, I released him from the firm. I did not want to be responsible for Jessie returning to prison.

Some speculations are involved in the following paragraphs.

I will always wonder if that unauthorized trip that Jessie made to the Bronx had anything to do with the two young African American men from the Bronx who later arrived in Elyria, Ohio, seeking employment at Erie Shores. Hindsight confirms that these two young African American men who possessed rare and unique computer skills would not just happen to come to a small city like Elyria, Ohio, seeking employment.

My research confirms, and I am now convinced, that Ron and Chris come to Elyria as undercover federal agents to gain employment at Erie Shores Computer to investigate Erie Shores and me because of the possible illegal activities of Jessie during that trip to the Bronx while driving the Erie Shores van. I not only hired these two young men, I eventually started an Internet firm (ESC Internet Services) and gave each of them a percentage ownership in the firm.

I was never informed about whether Jessie had made an illegal delivery to or from the Bronx with the Erie Shores van, but many of the actions of Ron and Chris during their employment at Erie Shores have led me to believe that Jessie had done something illegal, and that Erie Shores and I had been under surveillance during the entire time of Ron and Chris's employment. My biggest mistake was not filing charges against Jessie because this non filing made it appear that in whatever crimes Jessie committed in the Bronx, he was possibly acting on my behalf.

End of speculations.

CHAPTER THIRTY TWO

Prior to starting Erie Shores, I had already become involved in politics because of my position with the Urban League. One of my first partisan activities was to work with and support Dan Stringer, the democratic candidate for Lorain County prosecutor. The Republican candidate was Greg White, an attorney and ex-Marine who had served in Vietnam. White went on to win the Lorain County prosecutor's position, a position he would unfortunately hold for the next twenty years. Greg White ruled by putting fear and intimidation in the minds of most of the lawyers and defendants in Lorain County. My opposition to his campaign to become prosecutor was the beginning of a long-lasting adversarial relationship.

This adversarial relationship between Gregory White and me began around 1982. Our relationship became even more negative when Greg realized that we had the same mentors: Eric Nord and Scribner Fauver. Greg, Eric, and Scrib were Republicans, and I was a Democrat. But because of my very visible civic and business activities—started an Urban League affiliate in the county; started the first mainstream African-American-owned business in the county; was the first African American to serve on a bank board in the county; and did what would become many other "firsts" by an African American in the county—I became Eric's and Scrib's "favorite son." This meant that Eric and Scrib provided more attention and support in my endeavors than they provided to Greg in his county prosecutor's position.

═╫ ╫═

In 1985, after pressure from the few minority business persons in the county, the three democratic Lorain County commissioners, commissioned Virgil Mauntean, the county administrator, to develop a minority business program for the county. Virgil did not know where to begin in developing this program, so he called on me for assistance. I was more than glad to assist Virgil; after all, I was very familiar with the city of Cleveland's minority business program and just happened to have a complete copy in my office.

During that next six-month period, Virgil and I got to know each other quite well. The Lorain County minority business program was passed by the commissioners after the second reading. The program was now a part of the policies and procedures for public contracts in Lorain County.

Please keep in mind that the three Lorain County commissioners (Leonard Reichlin, George Koury, and Herbert Jacoby) were Democrats, and the county prosecutor, Greg White, was a staunch Republican. From the beginning of his tenure as county prosecutor, White did not like providing legal counsel to the three Democratic commissioners, and if the legislation or policies had anything to do with the advancement of African Americans, Hispanics, and Latinos, White was sure to be against those policies and legislation.

Up until 1986, Erie Shores Computer had not been included in the county's bidding process. My first opportunity to bid on a Lorain County sealed-bid contract came approximately five months after the passage of the county's minority business program.

The bid was too large for Erie Shores to bid as the prime contractor; therefore, Erie Shores bid as a subcontractor with a prime firm. The bid submitted by the Prime and Erie Shores was determined to be the second lowest in price, but the lowest bidder had refused to include the participation of a minority firm, thus making their bid "out of compliance." The three Democratic Lorain County commissioners were well aware of this noncompliance but decided to award the contract to this firm anyway.

I immediately called for a meeting with Virgil Mauntean, the county administrator. Virgil knew and admitted that the commissioners had acted improperly, but there was nothing he could do unless outside action was initiated. This was when I put my complaint in writing.

After my written complaint was ignored, I decided to threaten a civil lawsuit against the county. I knew White, the county prosecutor, would be required to defend the county commissioners. This was a lose-lose proposition for White because he disliked assisting the commissioners because they were all Democrats almost as much as he disliked assisting African Americans, Hispanics, and Latinos. His extra incentive to assist the commissioners in this situation was that this would be a fight against me and my firm.

Again I called on the wisdom of my friend Eric Nord. Eric wanted to be sure that I was willing to go through with a lawsuit against the county. After he was sure of my intentions, he directed me to his close friend, Attorney William Ginn, the partner at Thompson, Hine &

Flory in downtown Cleveland, Ohio. Eric did not trust any of the attorneys in Lorain County because he knew most of them were afraid to go up against Prosecutor White.

I met with Attorney Ginn, and he assigned two of his junior attorneys to my case. The meeting that brought fear to all three commissioners was held in the commissioner's hearing room. I had requested the assistance of my close friend Charles Hopkins, President and CEO of the Lorain County Community Action Agency.

When this meeting began, there was standing room only in a room with a capacity of approximately two hundred. Prosecutor White had underestimated me and my preparation for this session—a fact that he would remember fifteen years later. My two attorneys worked so well together that I nicknamed them Butch Cassidy and the Sundance Kid. They put White in numerous embarrassing situations during the two-hour session. I took the stand, and afterward, everyone in attendance, including the commissioners, knew that the county would lose this case if it proceeded to court. The final comment to me by Butch Cassidy and Sundance was how White's shoes had mud caked on, making it appear that he had been walking in a cow pasture. I could clearly tell because of his beet-red face that Prosecutor Gregory White was extremely angry about how the proceeding had gone.

A few days later, I was contacted by Commissioner Jacoby, requesting a meeting, but prior to this call, I had received a call from Vic Stewart, the chairman of the county's Democratic party. Vic requested that I join him for breakfast at the Holiday Inn that next morning. Upon arrival, I noticed that Mr. Stewart had a black male (whom I knew but had very little respect for) seated at the table with him. By the time this meeting was over, this black gentleman was no longer black; he had become the Negro who had attended this meeting to be Mr. Stewart's "Uncle Tom." Stewart posed the question: "Do you want to win a battle and lose the war?" I informed him that I was very disappointed at how the Democratic party continued to use minorities in Lorain County to advance the party's goals, and that minorities were not receiving anything for their support of the party. My last question to Stewart prior to my departure was, "Vic, you are a businessman; what would you do if someone had taken insurance clients from your firm?" The silence after my question confirmed that Vic understood my actions against the commissioners but did not approve of those actions.

My meeting with Commissioner Jacoby a few days after my breakfast with Vic was quite productive. Herb and I had developed a workable level of mutual respect, and this respect produced a productive outcome from our meeting. Jacoby's promise to me was that the commissioners would meet and discuss an appropriate financial amount that Erie Shores would receive for the contested contract, but I would be required to agree not to request participation in any portion of the contract. We ended the meeting agreeing to meet again within five days to cement a final agreement between Erie Shores Computer Inc. and the Lorain County government.

I had no problem giving up the Erie Shores portion of the contract as long as the amount of profit I had estimated to receive from the contract was in the settlement. I knew that I was in a position of power because Jacoby and the two other commissioners wanted to resolve this problem with as little fanfare and negative news as possible. The three Democratic commissioners also knew that Prosecutor White would be willing to use this division between the Democratic party and me as a positive for the county Republicans.

Within three days after my meeting with Commissioner Jacoby, Virgil Mauntean, the county administrator, called to inform me that the commissioners had an offer of settlement for Erie Shores. Virgil informed me that I would be meeting with him, as he would be representing the county commissioners. Later that same day, I met with Virgil in his office in the county administration building.

The Lorain County commissioner's offer was as follows:

Lorain County would agree to a settlement with Erie Shores Computer Inc. under the following conditions:

1. The outcome of the settlement would be final, with no future proceeding from either party.

2. Lorain County government would agree to pay Erie Shores Computer Inc. the total sum of $115,000.

3. As president and CEO of Erie Shores Computer Inc., I must agree to a "gag order" that would prevent me or any of my employees and or family members from discussing or sharing documents or information involved in the settlement.

I reviewed the settlement agreement with Butch Cassidy and Sundance, and they both agreed that the offer from the commissioners was a fair one and suggested that I accept it on behalf of Erie Shores. The next day I informed Virgil of my acceptance of the commissioner's settlement offer. Virgil stated that he would create the settlement agreement in final form for my signature within a couple of days.

When I received the $115,000 settlement payment, only $10,000 came from the county. The other $105,000 was paid to me by the two firms that had been awarded the contract. The following day, the article appeared in the *Chronicle* newspaper regarding the settlement. The article stated that the county had settled with Erie Shores Computer for $10,000. The commissioners had lied to the citizens of Lorain County about the settlement amount. Oh well,

I knew that Erie Shores had received a $115,000 settlement, and I could not tell anyone about the illegal activity of the commissioners and the county prosecutor due to the gag order.

⸻

Sometimes wisdom will tell you to, "leave well enough alone," but I did not adhere to this wisdom. I proceeded to agree to an action that Butch and Sundance suggested. This action, I am convinced, played an important role in my financial destruction almost fifteen years later. When I informed Butch and Sundance that the final agreement was ready for my signature, they suggested a final power play that would save them a trip to Lorain County and also piss Prosecutor White off one final time. Prosecutor Greg White had to travel to Butch and Sundance's offices in downtown Cleveland for my signature. Picture this: the county prosecutor, a staunch Republican and leader of his party, having to travel to Cleveland to have a document signed by a person whom he intensely disliked. And he had to perform this service representing three Democratic county commissioners, whom he also disliked.

Butch, Sundance, and I were awaiting the arrival of Prosecutor White in their firm's (Thompson, Hine & Flory) plush meeting room. Prosecutor White arrived and was escorted to the meeting room. We all knew each other, so there were no introductions and very little chitchat. Butch, Sundance, and I reviewed the agreement again, and I then signed a copy for my files and for the commissioner's files.

It was clearly apparent that Prosecutor White was quite uncomfortable in his surroundings and wanted to make his stay as brief as possible. After signatures were affixed and copies dispersed, my legal counsel asked me if there were any additional issues that needed answers. I looked at Prosecutor White and his face was now beet-red. As Prosecutor White appeared to stare through me, I asked him if there was a problem. White uttered only a few words prior to departing the office. The words uttered were, "I am going to get you."

After Prosecutor White's departure, Butch, Sundance, and I confirmed Prosecutor White's comment. After confirming what we had heard, both attorneys strongly suggested that I should be careful and stay as far away from Prosecutor White as possible and not to expect to participate in any future contracts for Lorain County.

━╬ ╬━

Life was good, and I felt the power of being rewarded for standing up for my rights against a powerful, unfeeling foe. After all, I had secured the backing and support of many of the members my Rotary Club. These were white businessmen between the ages of thirty-five and seventy-five years old.

Little did I know that this victory in 1987 against the county commissioners and the county prosecutor, would become a permanent lightning rod and vendetta against me by the county prosecutor. I am sure that I would have handled this victory in a more forgiving way if I had known the complete devastation my actions would bring to my family, my firm, and me fifteen years later.

I did not recognize it at the time, but 1987 was a year of major changes in my life. In addition to the ramped-up vendetta against me, my best friend and confidant, Charles Hopkins, drowned in Lake Erie. After Erie Shores was awarded the $115,000 settlement, I used approximately $15,000 of these funds to donate computers, printers, and software to the Elyria Ministerial Alliance.

CHAPTER THIRTY THREE

I met Charles Hopkins in the late 1970s. Charles was the president and CEO of the Lorain County Community Action Agency. This agency had approximately four hundred full-time employees. Charles and I were drawn to each other because of his wisdom and because of his desire and plans to enhance the lives of African Americans, Hispanics, and Latinos in Lorain County.

If progress for these minority groups was to take place, Charles and I knew that it would have to be through discrete and planned actions and activities through an agency or agencies already in operation—preferably agencies using federal and state funds to operate. We decided that his Lorain County Community Action Agency was the perfect vehicle to use to begin planning and developing the powerful changes needed for minority communities in Lorain County.

In order to update and keep the three communities updated and informed, the agency would hold monthly luncheons. These luncheons are where we gathered and shared information and ideas.

Then a special committee would meet on a regular basis and determine the various projects that would enhance the minority community. These projects would then be presented to the civic, political, and business communities by trusted agencies other than the Community Action Agency.

This special committee included: Charles Hopkins, Fannie Moore-Hopkins, Eddie Edwards, Rocky Ortiz, Carol Gordon, and Larry Jones. Two of the most important and successful projects ever undertaken by this luncheon group and special committee were: (1) how to maintain control of the Community Action Agency by making sure an African American or Hispanic was always in the leadership position; (2) how to gain control of the Lorain County Employment and Training Agency (ETA), formerly CETA.

Because of the plan instituted in 1984, an African American or Hispanic would lead the Community Action Agency for an additional twenty-seven years.

When the old Lorain County CETA program was changed to the Lorain County Employment & Training Program Agency, I was serving on its board. Charles and I were chosen to serve on the selection committee that would select the first ETA director. I will always remember how well Charles and I worked together for more than ten years to obtain our goals.

During the selection process, the field of candidates had been narrowed down to six. There was only one minority candidate out of six: an African American who had prior experience in the CETA program.

Charles and I were well aware that any of the six candidates would do a good job as the ETA director, but we wanted to be sure that this director would focus his or her attention on the communities where these services were most needed. We felt Bill would be that person.

Between the start of the selection meeting and our break for lunch, Bill's resume had been discussed and eliminated from the process. During our one-hour lunch, Charles and I met, and our focus was how to get his resume back into the selection process.

Our plan worked to a tee because by the time the selection process was complete, Bill's resume had not only been placed back into the selection process, but 100 percent of the selection committee had voted him in as the Employment and Training Agency's first director.

The luncheon committee of the Community Action Agency was elated at Bill's selection as director of the Employment and Training Agency. Bill turned out to be a great disappointment to the community he had promised to support. The feeling of betrayal and neglect were very strong in the African American, Hispanic, and Latino populations in Lorain County during his tenure of two decades.

⊶⊷

I remember the evening as if it were last year. Charles and his wife Fannie had joined Barbara and me for dinner at the Samurai Steak House in Beachwood, Ohio. I knew my good friend had not been feeling well for months, and I had also observed Fannie's concern about Charles.

After we had been seated in the Samurai for a few minutes, Charles asked me to accompany him to the restroom. After washing our hands, Charles commented, "Larry, if anything should happen to me, I want you and Barbara to take care of Fannie for me."

I immediately responded, "Hey, man, you can be assured that Fannie will be well cared for." I then stated to Charles, "Charles, if anything happens to me, I want you and Fannie to make sure Barbara is cared for." Charles promised.

Charles had been able to hide his diabetes from me and everyone else except his wife, Fannie. Fannie would later share that he had sworn her to secrecy concerning his health.

It was early one morning when the phone rang, and Fannie informed me that Charles had gotten out of bed while she was asleep and had left their condo without letting her know he was leaving or where he was going. Fannie's voice was trembling with fear when she shared that Charles had left his wallet, keys, and others personal items—items he had never left behind before.

It only took approximately thirty minutes to dress and travel from Elyria and arrive at Charles and Fannie's condo in Amherst. Fannie then shared with me that Charles had diabetes, and that the disease had gotten much worse during the past few months, causing him to become more and more depressed.

We both searched the wooded areas around the condos where they lived but with no luck. After about twenty minutes of searching, we arrived back at the condo.

I point blank asked Fannie if she thought Charles had done something to himself. Fannie looked at me and responded, "Larry, I am afraid he has; he would never leave the house like this."

We knew that we had to file a missing person report in the near future if we had not heard from Charles, but we would use the time until then searching and planning. At noon Fannie filed the missing-person report with the Lorain police department. By this time, Fannie and I were pretty sure that Charles had done something to harm himself. I now had to focus on comforting Fannie while attempting to keep some semblance of hope that Charles had just disappeared for a while.

In addition to comforting Fannie and praying that Charles would appear, I was well aware, as chairman of the Lorain County Community Action Agency's board of directors, that I would have to be prepared to inform the board of the status of its president and prepare them to go forward with the business of the agency.

The next morning Fannie received the devastating call from the Lorain police department, informing her that a body had been pulled from the waters of Lake Erie. The body could not be immediately identified because there was no identification on the body of the black male. Fannie was asked to come to the morgue to identify the body. Fannie called me immediately after identifying Charles.

I knew that I had to act extremely fast in my position as chairman of the Community Action Agency's board. I was well aware that Charles had been concerned about the finances of the agency, but what I did not know was the major negative financial report the board would hear at the upcoming board meeting.

I called an emergency meeting of the board for the following morning. Before the day was over, the news of Charles's drowning was on all television stations and in all the newspapers the next day.

All of the board members attended a special meeting, and the following happened:

1. I was asked to accept and accepted the position as the official spokesperson for the board until further notice. No other member would speak about the agency during this critical period; and no one did.

2. The board members were updated on the financial condition of the agency. The financial condition was so critical that the pending employee payroll was in jeopardy.

3. Charles's deputy, William Lock, was present at the meeting and in line to assume the duties of the agency, but I knew that there were a number of board members who had questions for Bill prior to a vote on him assuming the president's position. Knowing the importance of Bill being appointed to replace Charles, Bill and I met in the hall-way, where I strongly suggested that he respond in a tactful manner to the board members' questions. Bill answered the board members' questions and was voted in as the president of the Lorain County Community Action Agency.

4. The board had to immediately address the financial condition of the agency. Therefore, a special committee was appointed to meet with the executives of Lorain National Bank, the bank that held the agency's loans and various financial accounts. This was also the bank where Erie Shores had its corporate accounts.

5. Every board member wanted to know what had happened to Charles. Only three people would know the truth about what had happened to Charles. My official statement to the board at the meeting that day was that Charles had drowned accidentally in Lake Erie. I had assured Fannie that would be my official statement to the board at the meeting. Charles had kept the pain of living with severe diabetes as his long-time secret; therefore, Fannie and I were not about to taint or destroy his image and reputation.

Fannie and I also knew that the final report on Charles's death was not ours to confirm. The official confirmation would come from the county coroner. While we awaited the coroner's report, I asked Fannie to research the types of life insurance policies she and Charles had in place.

When Fannie called the insurance firm where Charles had his life insurance policy, she was informed that Charles had not paid on his policy in the past three months; therefore, the policy had officially lapsed. It took quite a bit of discussion with the agent, but, with prayer, the policy was reinstated. Fannie was now covered and in line to receive the payout from Charles's policy. She and I chalked up the nonpayment of the policy during those past months to Charles's mental state. We had dodged the first bullet, and now we needed to dodge the final one: the coroner's report. If he ruled Charles's death a suicide, Fannie would receive no payment from the insurance company.

I remember that morning so clearly when my cell phone rang, while on my way to Cleveland on I-90. It was the Lorain County coroner. He said, "Is this Larry?"

I said yes.

He said, "This is the coroner of Lorain County." (I prefer not to use the coroner's name in this book.) Larry, I am calling to let you know that I am in the process of completing the autopsy on Charles Hopkins. I understand that Mr. Hopkins was a very close friend of yours."

I said, "Yes, Charles was my closest friend."

There was, as I remember, as a long silence, but I am sure the silence was only for a couple of seconds. I was now waiting for the coroner to provide a preliminary ruling for Charles's death; instead, the coroner asked me a question: "Larry, my diagnosis on the manner of Charles's death will be completed today. I need to ask you a question: Do you have any reason to believe that Charles would commit suicide?"

I responded in an extremely positive voice: "No, I do not know of any reason Charles would want to commit suicide, and I am sure it was not suicide."

The coroner thanked me for my time, and we ended the call.

The next day the newspapers article read that Charles Hopkins, president and CEO of the Lorain County Community Action Agency had accidentally drowned in Lake Erie. I thanked God for what the coroner had done for my friend and his wife, Fannie.

Prior to that first board meeting after Charles's death, I received a call from my friend Stan Pijor, president of Lorain National Bank. Stan's call was to voice his concerns about the future of the agency without Charles's leadership. I assured Stan that the board would take the necessary actions that would be in the best interest of the agency and the bank, and that he would receive a prompt update after the board meeting.

After the board meeting, I called Stan and informed him that a special committee of the board needed to meet with him and his appropriate staff. The meeting was scheduled for that next morning.

Prior to the start of the meeting, I could see the concern on Stan's face. The committee updated the bank about the critical financial situation of the agency and stated that we would need to borrow funds to meet the upcoming payroll. The board assured the bank that the financial condition of the agency could and would be greatly improved within twelve to eighteen months.

Stan was well aware of the major critical roles the Community Action Agency played in Lorain County, so after many questions of the committee, Stan and the bank agreed to consider an additional loan to the agency. As members of the Community Action board were leaving the meeting room, Stan pulled me to the side and whispered that he needed to speak with me in private. We waited until all the committee members and bank staff (except the bank's executive vice president) left the room.

Stan concerns were more serious after the meeting than they were before the meeting. Stan looked into my eyes, continuing to hold my hand after the handshake, and posed this question: "Jones, are you confident that this agency can get its finances in order?"

I responded, "Yes Stan, I feel sure that the agency will get its finances in order."

Stan said, "Okay, Jones, I will extend this loan to the agency under one condition: that you remain on the agency's board for the next two years." I was serving my final term year at the time but agreed to remain on the board for the two additional years.

CHAPTER THIRTY FOUR

E rie Shores was doing well, and I had been researching the possibilities of expanding its operations, and I saw great opportunities for a Columbus, Ohio, office of Erie Shores. My daughter Tara
had come on board a few years prior and had proven to be a powerful and efficient vice president and an excellent decision maker. The
Columbus office would be hers to manage. The expansion was made,
and after a short period of time, Tara had developed the Columbus
office into the most profitable office in the company.

Around 1993, after four years of qualifying, Erie Shores was
awarded its 8(a) Minority Business Certification. This certification
allowed Erie Shores to bid independently on major government and
military contracts. Between 1995 and 1998, Erie Shores was awarded
numerous NASA contracts and one major military contract, worth
$36,000,000, from Wright-Patterson Air Force Base. In 1997 Erie
Shores Computer, Inc., was named, Small Business of the Year, in
Lorain County.

Even with all of my community responsibilities, I carved out time to assist Tara, Richard, and Pat in operating Erie Shores. Only years later would I realize that quality time with my family was what I had all but eliminated from my life.

⟩+ +⟨

There is no truer saying than this: a person's success draws the good, the bad, and the ugly. This is the beginning of my journey into hell— my introduction to a six-feet eight-inch, 320- pound business associate with a photographic memory who lived to do dark and evil things to others. Unknowingly, I permitted this evil person with a photographic memory, who was born to do evil, into my business operations and my personal life for more than five years! In my business operations, I used the valuable information and experience gained from my master's in guidance and counseling degree twice as much as my MBA studies, but the wisdom I gained and everything I learned from both of these degrees did not prepared me for my association with this sociopathic monster with the high IQ and the three others who would follow.

As I think on a regular basis about how this evil person was able to seed himself into my life and my business, I still have very few answers after fifteen years. This purely evil person was introduced to me in early 1998 by Reverend Carl P. Wallace, an ordained minister in the United Church of Christ. Being introduced to me by an ordained minister probably helped his entre.

Reverend Wallace was a young minister who also served as the Cleveland City Schools' minority business department manager. He was responsible for assuring that large Cleveland City School contracts contained minority business participation.

Erie Shores had been awarded numerous school contracts without the assistance of Reverend Wallace's department, but I welcomed any assistance the Minority Business Development Department could provide Erie Shores.

After I met Carl, I became impressed with his dedication and business professionalism. A few months after meeting Carl, he informed me that he wanted me to meet the other minority business owner doing business with the school system, Richard Buie. I told Carl that I would appreciated an introduction.

A couple of weeks later, Carl introduced me to Richard Buie. Buie's professionalism and manner of speech were what garnered my attention. Little did I know that almost everything Buie would say or do would be total plagiarism of someone else's words, actions, and accomplishments, and that this is how he had reached his present status and position. He had used and would continue to use this great gift (a photographic memory) that God had given him to do evil against everyone, including those who assisted him.

I guess it was only two to three months after our first meeting that I received a call from Buie around ten o'clock one evening. He had been arrested in his hometown of Shaker Heights, Ohio, for domestic violence against his wife. Buie needed someone to bail him out of jail. I did not think twice before driving the fifty miles to Shaker Heights, Ohio, to pay eight hundred dollars to bail my new business associate out of jail.

I never thought once about bailing Buie out of jail, even though I detested anyone who physically abused women, especially husbands abusing wives. Hindsight is twenty-twenty, and if I knew then what I would come to realize approximately seven years later, I would have let him remain in that jail cell. I had been provided a clear sign of his deceit earlier, when he illegally obtained a handicap parking pass and saw the enjoyment he felt about beating the system and not caring about using spaces of those who were really handicapped. I also know now that this big, sloppy six-foot eight-inch nobody had obtained special powers because he was a true sociopath. Instead of using this special gift of a photographic memory for good, he honed that gift to do evil.

Another early warning sign of Buie's evil was the way he treated his wife and divorced her after she had him arrested for beating her. He had a daughter who could not handle his sociopathic behavior, and for years, she had refused to associate with him. He spoke of her in negative ways and displayed no love or care for his daughter. I am sure the wife and daughter felt sorry for me because of the hell they knew I would experience from this business relationship.

This would be my first association with a sociopath. At the time I did not even know the definition of a sociopath. Fortunately, while serving as chairman of the Lorain County Board of Mental Health, I was taught the definition of the sociopath. If there are antichrists walking around on earth, I am sure Richard Buie met the definition attributed to a sociopathic antichrist. The evil he brought into my personal life and my business was devastating. He opened a portal where three more sociopaths were able to enter my business operations. Buie's evil was all consuming. He continued to use his photographic memory as a tool for evil instead of good. I tell myself over and over that I should have caught on to his lies and schemes, but I have come to the conclusion that his evil overwhelmed me and totally blinded me to an alternative thought process and to see or feel his evil.

I could not see this evil until long after it was too late to correct or prevent the horrific damage Buie had done and the damage he had permitted others to do to my businesses and to me and my family. I must admit that I received numerous warnings about Buie and others from those close to me, including my wife, Barbara, and my daughters, Tara and Galan. Again, I cannot explain to you or anyone else why I did not listen to or see the evil they had clearly seen in Richard Buie and later in Marty Conn, Dr. Arthur Boyd, and Dr. Merceda Perry.

Richard Buie's next move was to open a portal where Dr. Arthur Boyd Jr. and Dr. Merceda Perry would enter my company. Later he would bring Marty Conn into the business operations. If you speak with a psychologist about the sociopath, he or she will tell you that even one sociopath in your life can bring destruction; imagine having five sociopaths in your life over a four-year period.

CHAPTER THIRTY FIVE

My daughter Galan was approximately seven years old when I invited Dr. Arthur Boyd and Dr. Merceda Perry to stay overnight at my home instead of at the local motel. The next morning Galan came downstairs from her room and saw Drs. Boyd and Perry sitting at the kitchen island. She immediately returned to her upstairs room and asked her mother who those men were in our house. Barbara explained that they were daddy's friends.

I cannot explain Galan's actions, but from that day on for the next seven years, she had a special routine. The evening after she saw Boyd and Perry in our home, every night before she went to bed, she would make sure that all doors were locked and the window blinds were drawn. If we went to bed after she had gone to bed, many times Galan would call out to us and ask if we had locked the doors and had closed the blinds. I am convinced that Galan felt the evil in those two men when she saw them sitting in our house that morning, and her locking of doors and closing of blinds was a way to protect the family from the evil that she felt.

Barbara and I always felt Galan had a special ability to discern the good and evil in people she met. After Galan was born in 1992, Barbara decided that she would stay home with her for the first six months of her life. After five months we began searching for a babysitter for Galan so Barbara could return to work.

We were able to find two young ladies who we thought would do a good job with Galan. The first young lady was the daughter of a minister we knew. Barbara and I scheduled an appointment for Debbie to come over and become acquainted with Galan and us.

Debbie came in, and we settled in the living room area of the home. Barbara was holding Galan, and Debbie was sitting beside Barbara. I was seated on the sofa across from them. Barbara stood up holding Galan, and Debbie stood next to her. Barbara proceeded to hand Galan to Debbie, and as soon as Galan was in Debbie's arms she looked at Debbie, and fear came over her face, and she began to yell at the top of her voice while scrambling to get back to Barbara. As soon as Galan was back in Barbara's arms, she immediately quieted down. We waited for approximately five minutes and repeated the process with Debbie again holding Galan, and that same fear and yelling were repeated during the next four attempts. After that fourth attempt, we knew that Debbie would not become our babysitter.

Barbara and I were now concerned because we were wondering if Galan was going to agree to stay with anyone other than her mother. The problem was that Barbara had used up her six months of maternity leave.

That next week we invited another young lady over to meet Galan. We knew this was a critical meeting for us because if Galan reacted the same way she had the week prior, we would have a dilemma. Joyce arrived, and we repeated the identical process with her that we had performed with Debbie. Barbara stood and gave Galan to Joyce, and Galan looked at Joyce and gave her a big smile. Barbara and I could not believe it, but it was true. Galan permitted Joyce to hold her and showed no interest in getting back to Barbara. This was a great relief for us.

Barbara and I briefly discussed the stark difference in Galan's response to Debbie and to Joyce. We could not forget the fear we had seen on Galan's face each time Debbie had attempted to hold her.

CHAPTER THIRTY SIX

Over a four-year period Richard Buie and Marty Conn literally destroyed the operations of Erie Shores Computer. Buie was bold enough to use company funds that were supposed to be invested in his firm and used those investment funds to pay for his two sons' education at Ohio State University and for another son at Stanford University.

Erie Shores had been profitable since early in the third year of operations, but in 1999, because of the scams by Buie, Boyd and Perry, the company would suffer a loss. This small but frightening projected loss of approximately $154,000 would convince me to look seriously at the suggestion that Buie had talked about a few weeks prior: something about a Dr. Arthur Boyd Jr. that he knew in Shaker Heights who had a beverage firm and who was looking for someone to assist with the management of the firm. Buie stated that he met Boyd because their sons played on the Shaker Heights football team. Little did I know that my meeting Boyd was a well-planned meeting arranged by Buie and Boyd. I would not learn of Buie's scams until years later, after criminal charges had been filed against me.

I had shared the Erie Shores year-end losses with Buie, and he had seemed sincere about seeking avenues that would be profitable for Erie Shores. Again Buie suggested that I meet with this Dr. Arthur Boyd Jr., and I agreed to meet with him in late October of 1999.

I should have known that something was wrong when Dr. Boyd Jr. met with me in my office, and Buie did not attend the meeting. In addition, I should have known that it was not just a coincidence that Boyd appeared to know a little too many personal things about Barbara and me. He acted surprised when he realized that Barbara and I were from Durham, North Carolina, and that Barbara's sister, Esther, had married his long-time friend Sonny Amos. Boyd knew all about me and my firm and already had a detailed plan about how they were going to scam Erie Shores. Boyd knew that I would feel comfortable after realizing that he knew members of my family in Durham, North Carolina.

No matter what, the bottom line is that I know I am responsible for allowing these evil individuals into my personal life and the operation of my firm. The only consolation I have is my belief that the God Spirit has interceded on my behalf, and the punishment that they have experienced has been and continues to be extremely harsh.

CHAPTER THIRTY SEVEN

I n early 1998 Erie Shores Computer Inc. was the subcontractor on a major software bid awarded to Wang Lavatories (Wang Labs) by the Cuyahoga County, Ohio, Recorder, Mr. Frank Russo. I called it the $700,000 contract from hell.

Erie Shores provided computers and related products and services to the various Cuyahoga County departments for a number of years, and I was elated when Bud Atkins, the local Wang Labs salesman contacted me and inquired if Erie Shores would be interested in subcontracting with Wang Labs on a major software bid for the Cuyahoga County Recorder's office. Wang Labs was headquartered in Lowell, Massachusetts, and was one of the largest software developers in the nation; therefore, I was thrilled to be asked to subcontract with such a major software firm. Bud was the governmental salesman for Wang Labs. After being updated about the software responsibilities of Erie Shores in the bid for the Cuyahoga County Recorder's office, Bud scheduled a meeting with Bob Smith, his supervisor and Wang Lab regional sales manager.

Both Bob Smith and Bud Atkins were African American. After this brief meeting, where I signed the subcontracting contract with Wang Labs, I had no future contact with Bob Smith. For the next approximately four months, my only Wang Labs contact was Bud Atkins. Bud had been a sales representative at Wang Labs for a number of years and informed me that after this Recorder's project was completed, he was thinking of retiring and starting a home for troubled teen boys.

I provided the necessary information and pricing to Wang Labs for the Erie Shores portion of the bid. Approximately four weeks later, the bidding process was completed, and Wang Labs had won the software bid, with Erie Shores Computer as its subcontractor.

I immediately requested a meeting with Bud in order to obtain the work schedules for Erie Shores. A couple of days after my called to Bud, he and I met and I was informed that the Cuyahoga County Recorder, Mr. Frank Russo, needed some financial assistance for his campaign committee. This was my first time as a subcontractor where I had been informed that I needed to make a substantial donation to a campaign fund.

I informed Bud that neither Erie Shores nor I had the $3,000 to donate to the Russo campaign fund. Bud's response to me was, "Jones, you should view this donation as a loan because Erie Shores will be paid extremely well from this Recorder's Office software contract. With this assurance, I agreed to provide Bud a personal check for $3,000, made out to Frank Russo's campaign.

After providing Bud the check for Russo, approximately three weeks passed, and Bud had not contacted me as promised, so I called Bud and requested a meeting. I was becoming concerned because approximately three months had passed since the contract had been awarded to Wang Labs. After three calls to Bud, he responded and informed me that he needed to meet with me.

The next day Bud and I met at a restaurant in Cleveland, on St Clair Avenue. I asked Bud why we had not begun the implementation of the Wang Labs software that had been created for the Recorder's Office. This was when Bud dropped the bomb on me that would cause a continuous explosion for the next two and a half years.

Bud calmly informed me that Wang had not developed any software for the Cuyahoga County Recorder's Office. He went on to say that I should not worry because County Recorder Frank Russo was aware that no software had been developed when the contract was awarded to Wang Labs.

I asked Bud what the hell he was talking about. Bud told me to calm down because Frank was in control of the project, and he would give Wang Labs and Erie Shores plenty of time to develop the software. Erie Shores was now between a rock and a hard place because I had provided Russo $3,000 and Erie Shores was under contract, secured by a performance bond for software work to be performed in the Cuyahoga County Recorder's Office.

Little did I know at the time that Frank Russo had been secretly promised and assured that he would be appointed to the position of Cuyahoga County Auditor. The present auditor would be moving on to another position. During our next meeting was when Bud dropped this second bombshell on me. He said that Frank had decided to accept the position of Cuyahoga County Auditor and would be resigning as the Cuyahoga County Recorder. Again, Bud assured me that everything was under control. Frank had sent word through Bud that I should not worry about the changes that were happening because his successor would be a person he had handpicked. This handpicked person was Joe O'Malley. I was assured that Joe understood the software situation very well and would continue the software process Frank Russo had started.

Bud instructed me to begin communicating directly with Joe O'Malley, and on February 28, 2000, I sent Joe my first written correspondence. Joe O'Malley never responded to my correspondence because he would never be appointed Cuyahoga County Recorder.

A couple of weeks prior to the public announcement of Russo's appointment as the new Cuyahoga County Auditor, Bud informed me that all was well, and that Joe O'Malley was sure to be the next Cuyahoga County Recorder.

Frank Russo became the Auditor for Cuyahoga County as planned, but Joe O'Malley did not become the next Cuyahoga County Recorder. Frank Russo's plan had not gone well in securing Joe O'Malley a position as the Cuyahoga County Recorder. What Frank and his political group had not taken into account was the secret plans of another powerful faction of the Cuyahoga County Democratic party.

When all the dust settled, Joe O'Malley had lost out to this guy named Patrick O'Malley, no kin to Joe. I had heard of Patrick O'Malley because of Erie Shores' prior contracts with the city of Cleveland. My technology people had interfaced with Tony Ma, who served as Patrick O'Malley's director of technology in the city of Cleveland Recorder's office.

Upon learning that Joe O'Malley would not become the Cuyahoga County Recorder, I placed a call to Bud Atkins to find out what this new appointment would mean for the Recorder's software contract. After numerous calls to Bud with no response, I knew problems were brewing.

I had enough knowledge of Patrick O'Malley to know he was an asshole who loved the limelight and always wanted to be in control. Patrick O'Malley stood approximately five feet six inches tall and truly suffered from the short-man syndrome.

After Bud Aitkin finally agreed to meet, the update he provided chilled me to my soul. He was no longer attempting to sugarcoat anything that was happening. Bud informed me that Frank's plan to have the Democratic central committee name his guy Joe O'Malley had been overpowered by the people who wanted Patrick O'Malley in the Recorder's position. When I asked where the software situation stood, Bud stated that he did not know because Frank Russo and Patrick O'Malley were political enemies.

To make a long story short, Wang Labs and Erie Shores was now on their own regarding the software for the Cuyahoga County Recorder's office—software that did not exist.

After this meeting with Bud, I immediately placed a call to the Wang Lab headquarters. From the numerous departmental transfers, it became clear that the corporate office personnel were not familiar with the Cuyahoga County Recorder's project.

After finally speaking with one of the sales managers and the software manager and explaining that I had been informed by Bud Atkins that Wang Labs had not even developed the software package that was sold to the Cuyahoga County Recorder's Office, I was convinced they knew little to nothing about this contract. I was now pretty sure that this software contract for the Cuyahoga County Recorder's office had been created and managed and controlled by Frank Russo along with Bob Smith and Bud Atkins, the two local Wang Labs sales personnel. I would later find out that shortly after my conversation with Bud Atkins, he resigned from Wang Labs.

After my conversation with the managers at Wang, I attempted to reach Frank Russo via phone for approximately two weeks but received no response. This was another confirmation that Erie Shores was in trouble concerning this contract. That $3,000 payment to Bud for Frank's campaign was the main reason I did not file charges against Cuyahoga County. I knew that I was breaking the law when I provided that much money to Frank Russo's political campaign. With the evidence that I now had about this software scam, and having evidence that Wang's corporate personnel were not even aware of this software contract, I should have notified the authorities.

CHAPTER THIRTY EIGHT

Patrick O'Malley became the new Cuyahoga County Recorder and was moving into his new office. One of his first official actions after moving in was to replace the entire staff that had served under Frank Russo.

O'Malley's next order of business was to review all of the major projects that Frank had started or had planned to start. The largest project was the new software that had been developed for the Recorder's office. I knew I would be receiving a call from Patrick or Tony Ma, the Recorder's new technology manager. Tony Ma had served in this same position for O'Malley while O'Malley was the Recorder for the city of Cleveland. When the call came, I was not asked, but ordered, to attend a critical meeting at the Recorder's office.

After the summons by Patrick O'Malley himself, I quickly called Wang Lab headquarters to alert them of the call I had received from O'Malley. I was informed that Wang had also received the same type of call from Patrick O'Malley. The sales manager strongly suggested to me that I should not speak directly with Mr. O'Malley or any of his representatives after that day. He said that as the subcontractor for Wang Lavatories on the software contract, I would be required to follow the professional and legal guidance of Wang Labs. I was informed that I would be receiving a call from Wang's legal department within a couple of days because a representative from their legal department would be representing Wang at this meeting with Patrick O'Malley. Knowing that Wang would have its lawyer there gave me some comfort that Erie Shores would also have some legal representation and protection; after all, Erie Shores was a subcontractor of Wang.

I met with Richard Brown, the Erie Shores' executive vice president to update him on the meeting scheduled to take place that next Monday afternoon at the Cuyahoga County Recorder's office. Richard would need to accompany me to this meeting just in case any technical questions were posed. I wanted Richard there also because I was feeling more and more distrustful of Wang Labs and its questionable support for Erie Shores Computer.

Monday morning came in a flash, and Richard and I traveled to Cleveland Hopkins Airport where we awaited the arrival of Attorney Jack Coates, who was flying in from Wang Labs' headquarters. Arrangements had been made for him to ride with us to the Recorder's meeting. On our way from the airport, after brief introductions, Jack reminded me that it would be critical for him to do all of the talking in the meeting because he was there to represent Wang Labs and Erie Shores Computer.

Attorney Coates was an interesting guy: from his western outfit, including his cowboy hat, to his southwestern accent. He made it very clear that Wang Labs was not entering this meeting with any fear or concern about any legal actions by the Recorder's office.

The three of us arrived at the Recorder's office and were seated in the conference room. As we had discussed on our ride from the airport, O'Malley would probably let us sit for a while after arriving, just to show that he was in charge of the meeting, and this was exactly what happened. O'Malley entered the room approximately fifteen minutes after our arrival. I was seated on the side, at the far end of the conference table, and Richard was seated in the chair to my right. Jack took the first chair on the left, next to the other end, where O'Malley would be seated.

O'Malley began the meeting by informing all of us, including his technology manager, Tony Ma, that he wanted to know what was going on with this software project, and if he was not satisfied with the answers he received, the Recorder's office would immediately file a lawsuit against Wang Labs and Erie Shores Computer. He stated that he had been made aware that the software package was purchased by Frank Russo, while County Recorder, and that it appeared that this software did not exist. If this software did not exist, he would not only file against Wang and Erie Shores but he would file charges against Frank Russo also.

I would guess O'Malley's ranting and raving, all while standing, went on for at least six or seven minutes. I had mentioned to Coates about O'Malley's short-man syndrome while driving from the airport.

All of a sudden, while O'Malley was talking, Coates stood to his feet, standing approximately six feet three inches tall, and stated in a low but very clear and authoritative voice, "Mr. O'Malley, I have flown in this morning from Boston, Massachusetts, to a meeting that you called. It appears from your comments that you have decided to sue my firm and Erie Shores Computer. If this is the case, we might as well end this meeting now; but if you called this meeting to resolve the problem with our software, then I suggest we get on with the business at hand. Oh, by the way, I strongly suggest we work to resolve these issues instead of threatening a lawsuit because I have approximately fifty lawyers in my office who are inactive, and I am sure they would love to demonstrate to you how they can defend a case such as this, for at least two and maybe three years."

Patrick O'Malley stood in silence for a few seconds after Coates completed his comments but quickly took his seat, as though he had been chastised by a parent. O'Malley watched Coates closely as Coates directed every word at him, as he towered over the seated O'Malley.

O'Malley quickly realized that this meeting was no longer in his control. He also had become aware that, as the new Recorder, he was not in a position to begin his tenure with a lawsuit that could last for months or even years.

Attorney Coates knew that he had assumed control of this meeting and proceeded to present the details of his firm's plans about how to resolve the Recorder's software problems. Coates was presenting a plan to the Recorder's office that had not been presented to Erie Shores; therefore I was hearing this plan for the first time, along with O'Malley. Coates's presentation began to give me great concern because he nor his firm had considered Erie Shores Computer important enough to share the Wang Labs plan prior to its presentation to the Recorder's office.

The Wang Labs plan presented by Coates was basic. Coates admitted that Wang Labs did not have the software developed as had been stated in its contractual agreement during the bidding process. To correct this problem, Wang would agree to commit one of its lead software developers full time, in the development of this software. Coates, without my approval, then promised that Erie Shores would commit one of its software developers on a full-time basis also. Upon hearing this commitment for Erie Shores without my prior approval, I almost jumped out of my seat but knew that my actions would reveal a lack of togetherness of Erie Shores and Wang Labs. This could not happen because I continued to be pretty sure that Erie Shores would be in a better position working with Wang Labs against O'Malley than against Patrick O'Malley on its own.

Coates continued with his offer to Patrick O'Malley by stating that Wang Labs would, as a show of good faith, sign the ownership of Wang Labs' "Software Source Code" over to the Cuyahoga County Recorder's Office and to Erie Shores Computer to be owned equally. Richard and I clearly understood the importance and value of owning 50 percent of this software source code. I was now feeling much better about Coates and his presentation.

Attorney Coates ended his approximately ten-minute presentation by stating that his firm would need an answer from O'Malley within five days, and that he would alert his legal team to be ready for legal proceedings if his offer was rejected. O'Malley stared at Coates for a few seconds and adjourned the meeting without any verbal response to Coates. It was extremely clear that this meeting had not gone as O'Malley had planned because now he was showing anger and fear.

I was shocked at the way Coates had pretty much disrespected O'Malley in the presence of everyone at this meeting. As we departed the building, Coates was quiet as he walked toward the parking garage ahead of Richard and me. This was clearly a sign that he did not want to discuss the actions he had just taken in that meeting—actions he had not discussed or mentioned to me. I was not concerned about his silence while walking because we would be driving him back to the airport for his return flight to Boston.

Once in the car, Coates's first comment was an apology for not in-forming me of his plans prior to the meeting. He explained that the reason for not informing me was because he wanted all of the pres-sure and responsibility to be directed toward Wang Labs and not Erie Shores. I bought his reasoning hook, line, and sinker, not realizing that he nor Wang gave a damn about Erie Shores Computer.

Coates stated during the ride that he was positive O'Malley would accept his offer because he was a frightened little man who wanted to be more than he was. Coates would have the offer agreement mailed to both O'Malley and me for signatures.

I received, reviewed, and signed my copy of the proposed soft-ware development agreement approximately six business days after our meeting with O'Malley. I knew that even with this signed agree-ment, if there were any problems with O'Malley, Erie Shores had the technical and legal support and backing of the powerful Wang Labs, so I felt I had put Erie Shores in as strong a position as possible with the Recorder's office.

⪥⪤

Approximately two weeks later I received a copy of the signed agree-ment for my records. O'Malley had indeed agreed to and signed the agreement. Approximately two days later I received a call from O'Malley's executive assistant, informing me that a meeting had been scheduled for the next morning at his office—a meeting that my software developer and I were expected to attend. A few days pri-or, Richard and I had received a call from Steve. Steve introduced himself and informed us that he had been hired by Wang as the Independent software Contractor that would work with Erie Shores in the development of the Recorder's office software. Steve and Richard had spoken briefly via phone, and he had informed Richard that he was a Canadian citizen living in the United States and working on software projects for a couple of firms, including Wang Labs. I would not become aware until a few weeks later of the importance of Wang hiring an independent foreign software contractor to develop this software.

Richard and I arrived at O'Malley's office for the 9:00 a.m. meeting, expecting to meet Steve for the first time. O'Malley's executive assistant was a blonde, approximately thirty-five years of age. It was clear that she had assumed her boss's overbearing personality. Richard, Steve, and I were seated in the conference room where O'Malley had received his royal ass kicking. Tony Ma arrived approximately ten minutes after we were seated, and O'Malley, as he had done for our last meeting, arrived about seven minutes after Ma's arrival.

I was not ready for the level of disrespect and hell that O'Malley had planned for Erie Shores and Steve. The first thing O'Malley did was to make it very clear that he was now in charge and in control of this meeting and all future meetings related to the development of this software. He totally disrespected my position as owner and president of Erie Shores and threatened to sue Erie Shores at any point in the future if the software was not completed. Again, I held my anger in order for Richard and Steve to have their meeting with Tony Ma and get started with the software development.

I knew O'Malley had made threats that should not have been made, so upon my return to my office, I placed a call to Attorney Coates at Wang to provide an overview of the threats O'Malley had made. Coates was in meetings, and I was informed that he would return my call as soon as he had the opportunity.

Approximately two hours later, Coates returned my call. As I began to update him on the morning meeting with O'Malley, he interrupted me and said, "Jones, I can no longer speak with you concerning the Cuyahoga County Recorder's software contract. I have just returned from a corporate meeting where it was announced that Wang Labs is in the process of being sold to a firm outside of the United States."

What I had heard wasn't something my brain could readily process immediately because the level of shock and fear those words had brought was totally overwhelming. During my period of inability to speak, Coates added that it was now the responsibility of Erie Shores and the independent software contractor to fulfill the Recorder's software requirements. "Jones, I wish you good luck working with O'Malley." I cannot recall if I gave any response to Coates after his devastating news. That was my final conversation with Coates or any other employee of Wang Labs. I had permitted Wang Labs, the prime contractor of this contract, to transfer all of the responsibility for this software project to Erie Shores Computer and a foreign independent contractor.

I knew prior to this devastating news that working with Patrick O'Malley would be one of my biggest business challenges thus far. A confrontation with this guy could put Erie Shores Computer out of business, and I was well aware that Patrick O'Malley did not give a damn about the future of my firm. I would learn from Tony Ma and a few other managers throughout the city of Cleveland and Cuyahoga County government that O'Malley had made a number of enemies in high places, but no one wanted to take O'Malley on or confront him. Knowing this concerned me even more because this information confirmed that I had no one in the city of Cleveland or Cuyahoga County government that I could confide in or report any abuse to by O'Malley—abuse I was certain would come.

⊷ ⊶

I had no choice but to assign Richard, my executive VP and top technology guru, full time in the development of this Recorder's software. The loss of Richard's technical guidance and leadership during the next two-year period would be devastating to Erie Shores.

The projected time it would take to complete the software had been estimated at between five and seven months, but because of the approximately fifteen changes that O'Malley forced Richard and Steve to make, the project lingered on for almost two years. During those two years O'Malley refused to pay Erie Shores for any of the fourteen hundred man hours Richard had invested in the software development.

Even though O'Malley refused to pay Erie Shores the $153,000 due for Richard's work, I knew I was still holding an ace card: Erie Shores Computer owned 50 percent of the source code from which the Recorder's office software was being written. This meant that Erie Shores would be in a position to obtain royalty payments from the use of this software.

During one of my weekly meetings with Richard, he informed me that O'Malley had brought another outside software firm in and O'Malley had instructed Richard and Steve to provide various technical information to these developers. From the information requests of these programmers, Richard deduced that O'Malley had brought them in to rewrite the source code for the software that Richard and Steve had spent almost two years developing.

Once Richard alerted me of the actions of these programmers, I knew that O'Malley had found a way to take away my ace in the hole—Erie Shores' 50 percent ownership of the software source code. O'Malley and the Recorder's Office owed Erie Shores Computer $153,000, and now he was also eliminating from the Recorder's software the software source code in which Erie Shore had a 50 percent ownership.

I had already complained to the Cuyahoga County commissioners about the nonpayment of the Erie Shores Computer invoices. The commissioners never addressed or responded to any of my requests for payment.

CHAPTER THIRTY NINE

By this time I needed to locate information that I could maybe use to convince O'Malley to pay Erie Shores for the work it had performed; therefore, I decided to do some investigative research on Mr. O'Malley. In my opinion, he had too much authority in the county government. For some unknown reason, he had also displayed this extraordinary power while in his Recorder's position with the city of Cleveland.

I remembered, while completing the documents to become certified as a minority business for the city of Cleveland, that one of the questions on the form had appeared to be a very odd question. This question focused on whether the applicant had done business with or had been affiliated with any member of the Irish Republican Army, (IRA).

Patrick O'Malley was a pure asshole, and everyone around him knew that fact. I could tell from statements in meetings that some knew of the hell O'Malley had put Erie Shores through. One thing

O'Malley did not expect was someone having the ability to view his personal and confidential files that were stored on his personal office system. Erie Shores had one individual with these technical abilities.

After O'Malley had stolen the software source code from Erie Shores, my technical expert began to search and research any and all information O'Malley had on his office system. Viewing information on his system would not be very hard to do because O'Malley had loaded the Recorder's software on his personal office system in order for the firm that was changing the software source code to be able to keep him personally updated.

I needed to locate something in those files that would make O'Malley think twice before continuing to refuse to pay Erie Shores. Files were found that appeared to be activities associated with the Irish organization called Sinn Fein and possibly the Irish Republican Army, (IRA)

After viewing some of these personal documents, I decided that it would be in my best interest and Erie Shores' best interest if I no longer pursued the $153,000 owed to Erie Shores, nor would I attempt to sue the county over the source code theft.

I knew that if I had discovered these documents and information on O'Malley, there was an excellent chance that the FBI also knew something about these documents and was probably monitoring O'Malley. I decided to donate the few additional days of time remaining to complete Erie Shores' part of the software, knowing that Erie Shores would never perform any future work for the Cuyahoga County Recorder's office. It was my plan never to come in contact with O'Malley again.

I never saw O'Malley again, but a few years later I began to read about him in the *Cleveland Plain Dealer* newspaper. O'Malley and his estranged wife had been having domestic problems and it appeared that somehow, the FBI had gained access to information on his home computer. The public story was that the FBI found child pornography on O'Malley's system. O'Malley was charged and sentenced to time in a federal prison camp.

⇥ ⇤

My Speculation Derived from Factual Information

Now please permit me to share with you what I think really happened to Patrick O'Malley and what he did for the FBI and why he received only a slap on the wrist instead of an extremely long prison sentence. I assure you, many pieces of an interesting puzzle will fit into place after you read what comes next.

It appears that the FBI had been investigating Patrick O'Malley's association and activities related to the Irish Republican Army (IRA) for a period of time. These investigations were ongoing while O'Malley held his position as Recorder for the city of Cleveland and continued after becoming the Cuyahoga County Recorder.

It also appeared that O'Malley knew about and possibly participated in the ongoing corrupt political activities of government and business officials who held top positions in both the city of Cleveland and Cuyahoga County. These individuals knew they could depend on each other to keep quiet about their illegal dealings because each one had as much to lose as the other.

What the others involved in these illegal activities didn't know was that Patrick O'Malley was being investigated because of his activities related to an international terrorist organization, the IRA, while covering as work with Sinn Fein. The FBI began investigating the businesses that had been awarded contracts with the city of Cleveland and Cuyahoga County governments. Erie Shores was one of those firms because of its contracts with the city of Cleveland and its subcontract with the firm that was developing the Cuyahoga County Recorder's software.

It appeared that the FBI decided the time had come to take action against O'Malley. They were aware of O'Malley's marital problems and his pornography obsession. The FBI used the estranged-wife of O'Malley to seize his computer. This was how federal charges for possession of child pornography were brought against O'Malley. I am pretty sure the Feds had been monitoring O'Malley's trips to Ireland for a number of years, attempting to discern if his activities were related to Sinn Fein or to the Irish Republican Army, (IRA) or both.

The feds made sure the child porn charges against O'Malley made all of the media outlets, and indeed these charges against Patrick O'Malley became a public spectacle.

The documents observed would lead one to believe that O'Malley was really arrested for his activities related to his out-of-country activities. O'Malley knew that he had to do something to avoid prosecution that could send him to prison for many years, even for life. The feds also knew that the status and appearance of the IRA were changing from being viewed as a terrorist organization. This is when, through his attorneys, O'Malley played his major ace cards.

Patrick O'Malley had been involved in the dirt and, therefore, had the dirt on Jimmy Demoria, Frank Russo, and other top-level public officials in county and city government and on some of the businesspeople doing business with the county and city. He shared this explosive information with the feds to save his life. O'Malley knew that he had to give the FBI something so massive and critical that the authorities would have no choice but to begin serious negotiations with him.

A few months later, the public began seeing articles about various top-level Cuyahoga County and City of Cleveland officials being investigated. O'Malley pled guilty to the charges brought against him for child pornography—first-time federal charges that would have given him up to ten years for a first offense. For his information, O'Malley was sentenced to a federal prison camp for fifteen months.

Over the next seven years more than fifty top city of Cleveland, Ohio, and Cuyahoga County, Ohio, politicians, city and county managers, judges, and numerous business owners were charged in federal and state court and sentenced to state and federal prison terms; heading the list were Jimmy Demoria and Frank Russo. My long time adversary, Gregory White was the US Attorney and the lead prosecutor in these activities.

Patrick O'Malley, after serving his extremely light sentence, returned to the Northern Ohio area and was eventually awarded custody of his two children and reinstated by the Ohio Bar Association.

I believe this information will shed more light on how the feds became aware of the information and documents that would lead to the indicting and convicting of the largest number of Ohio city and county government officials, court officials and businesspersons ever, in the history of Ohio.

End of Speculation

CHAPTER FORTY

I was totally convinced that Richard Buie was a business associate that I could put great trust in. After all, I had assisted his firm with subcontracts and bailed his big ass out of jail when his wife filed charges of domestic abuse against him in Shaker Heights, Ohio. How was I to know at that time that a sociopath with a photographic memory had entered my life and would become the portal for three more sociopaths to enter my personal and business life? I have replayed this five-year saga over and over in my mind a million times, and I remain convinced that with all of the precautions taken, I was not even close to seeing the evil powers that Buie possessed. It was amazing how he was able to convince me that he was a good guy while at the same time putting a process in place that would destroy me, my firm, and the finances of my family and business. I guess all I can say to you is: if you have ever had a sociopath in your life, you may be able to somewhat understand.

It was now early 1999, and I was comfortable with my relationship with Buie and including him in my top-level business meetings. I was keeping him abreast of the problems Erie Shores was experiencing with Patrick O'Malley and the Cuyahoga County Recorder's office. He was also aware of the major contract with the city of Cleveland that Erie Shores was bidding.

Buie had mentioned that this Dr Boyd Jr. was a medical doctor and also owned a beverage firm. His third mention of Dr Boyd Jr. was to inform me that Dr Boyd Jr. was searching for someone to help him manage the beverage firm that he and his partner had incorporated because he wanted to focus more on his medical career.

I agreed to meet with Dr. Arthur Boyd Jr. through the recommendation of Richard Buie, not knowing about the evil intentions of both men or about how they would use the family information to lure me into a false level of comfort. At this point I was feeling good about meeting Dr. Boyd. After all, he was being introduced to me through a trusted business associate. Additionally, the person I was scheduled to meet was an African American medical doctor! This not only provided a level of comfort, it also instilled a high level of trust.

When Dr. Boyd and I met in my office, Buie did not attend. I thought briefly that this was unusual, but when I mentioned this to Buie later, his response was, "I wanted the two of you to get to know each other, without me being present." Boyd seemed in a hurry to share his background with me. I soon learned that he was born in Durham, North Carolina, my hometown. He would wait until later in the approximately forty-minute meeting to use the family connection. I had a picture of my family on the windowsill, in plain view. He noticed it and asked about my wife's family. I shared that Barbara's maiden name was Keith. This was when he could have won an Oscar. He played the extremely excited role and said, "Larry, is your sister-in-law's name Esther?" Of course, this caught me by surprise, and I commented yes. He went on to say something like, "Man, this is a small world," and shared that Sonny, Esther's husband, had been his best friend since childhood. Dr. Boyd went on to state how he now understood why we were destined to meet. I was now feeling a high level of comfort about Dr. Boyd and the possibility of assisting him with his beverage firm, Star Beverage Inc., Delaware.

Dr. Boyd could tell their (Buie's and his) plan was working, so he proceeded with his spiel about Star Beverage Inc. of Delaware. Boyd went on to tell me lies about Star Beverage, its seventeen-million-dollar value and how he needed someone with my management abilities to assist with the management of the firm, because he lacked the management knowledge and also because he wanted to focus more on his medical career. He shared that he had a partner, Dr. Merceda Perry, also a medical doctor, whom he had met and befriended while in medical school at MeHarry Medical College. Boyd left the best for the last part of the meeting. He showed a large photo of himself and three other doctors posing in their bloody garb after a surgery—a surgery that I would later learn was performed as an unlicensed doctor in a Latin American country.

He then shared that Star Beverage had won a beverage contract with the US Navy worth $69,000,000. I must admit, this really piqued my attention. Dr. Boyd and I agreed that we would hold another meeting that would also include Dr. Perry and Buie, and a copy of the $69,000,000 contract would be available for viewing at the meeting.

Approximately two weeks later, the four of us (Buie, Boyd, Perry, and I) met at the Sheraton Airport Hotel, located at the Cleveland Hopkins International Airport. Dr. Perry had flown in from Greensboro, North Carolina. Buie informed me that he had performed in-depth due diligence on Dr. Boyd, Dr. Perry, and Star Beverage Inc. of Delaware. I relied on the report that Buie provided me. Prior to this meeting, Buie and I had met, and we had agreed that I would assist in the management of Star Beverage, and that he would assume the title of sales manager if we could come to a contractual agreement. Of course, we reached an agreement, the agreement that would turn my sixteen years of financial success and the family personal finances into total disaster.

If I had performed my own background checks and not relied on Richard Buie to perform the background checks on Boyd, Perry, and Star Beverage of Delaware, I would have easily uncovered the following:

A. Star Beverage of Delaware had no assets.
B. There were at least three additional Star Beverages in business, all incorporated by Boyd and his wife.
C. Neither Boyd nor Perry had any personal assets.
D. I would not have relied on FirstMerit Bank to perform the only additional due diligence and background check on Boyd, Perry, and Star Beverage of Delaware.
E. I would have known about the numerous scams Boyd had performed against more than eight individuals and two firms.
F. I would have uncovered the fact that the $69,000,000 contract that Star Beverage Inc. of Delaware had with the US Navy was fraudulent.
G. I would have known about the numerous frivolous lawsuits that Boyd had filed and the active lawsuits pending against him.
H. I would have known about Boyd not being able to pass the medical exam, even after taking the test in fifteen states.
I. I would have known about Boyd being incarcerated for thirty days for attempting to bribe the Michigan medical test examiner to provide him the answers to the test.
J. I would have known about Boyd having performed more than two hundred illegal surgeries at the University of Maryland's Trauma Center.

K. Barbara and I would never have signed for the two major loans to Star Beverage in the amounts of $1,600,000 and $400,000.

L. Erie Shores would have never agreed to purchase more than $950,000 worth of beverage-production equipment.

M. Erie Shores would never have cosigned for the building Star Beverage would lease in Elyria, Ohio.

N. I would have never introduced Boyd and Perry to the mayor and the entire city council of Elyria.

I am positive that it would not have been very difficult to have uncovered some of these activities of Boyd, even if I had performed my own background checks; but I depended on my business associate and friend, Richard Buie, and more importantly, I depended on the executives of FirstMerit Bank, who failed in performing their due diligence prior to approving two loans to Star Beverage Inc., Delaware, totaling $2 million.

I have asked myself a million times how the executives of FirstMerit Bank, a large regional bank where I was a member of its board of directors, could have performed such poor due diligence. Also, how could a business associate to whom I had given so much assistance commit such cold and calculating scams against me and my company?

CHAPTER FORTY ONE

I introduced Boyd and Perry to the executive management at FirstMerit Bank, the bank where I had been a member of its board of directors for a number of years. As a member of FirstMerit's board, I felt that it was important that I used another bank to finance the needs of Erie Shores Computer. That bank was Huntington National Bank.

I had served as a member of Premier Bank's board prior to serving on the FirstMerit board, so when FirstMerit purchased Premier, I was asked to serve on its board. Bruce Stevens, the vice president of the business loan department at Premier Bank was hired as FirstMerit's executive vice president of its business loans department. Bruce was also active in the community and had accepted my offer to serve on the Urban League's board of directors.

I am positive that if Bruce had not put so much confidence in our friendship and had performed the normal due diligence on Boyd,

Perry, and Star Beverage, the two major loans would not have been awarded to Star Beverage Inc. of Delaware and these two scam artists.

It appears that the first time Bruce had any idea there was a problem with the loans was when he received a letter from Dr. Boyd, approximately eight days after the Star Beverage loans had been approved, stating that he, Boyd, had not signed for the loans. A few days later, the loan problems were confirmed when Boyd and Perry arrived, unannounced, at the FirstMerit headquarters in downtown Elyria. They were there in an attempt to have the balance of the $1,600,000 loan transferred from the Star Beverage of Delaware account to different Star Beverage firm's accounts that Boyd owned.

Bruce placed a call to me to alert me that Boyd and Perry were at the bank attempting to transfer the Star Beverage Inc., Delaware loan funds. His question was whether I was aware of this transfer, and I told him no and that I would arrive at the bank within a few minutes. Intimidation was the main tool of Boyd and Perry. They knew how to frighten and intimidate businesspeople, especially white businesspeople and bankers especially. Unfortunately, Bruce was very intimidated by Boyd and Perry, and they knew this and would use this tool against Bruce and other FirstMerit Bank executives over and over during the next eighteen-month period.

After arriving at FirstMerit, I confronted both Boyd and Perry and asked them what they were doing in Elyria and, more importantly, at the bank. My question was rhetorical because Bruce had already informed me that their visit had been an attempt to transfer funds from the Star Beverage account. They would have been successful if it had not been for the quick thinking of the cashier. The cashier quickly alerted Bruce (a) because she had not seen these men in the bank before and (b) because they were black. This was one time when I totally approved of profiling.

Of course, Boyd and Perry denied their attempt to transfer funds from the legitimate Star account. The four of us met in one of the adjacent conference rooms. I knew I could no longer trust these so-called African American medical doctors, and I wanted out of the loan agreement. This was when I should have involved Bruce's supervisor in this situation because I was now observing what appeared to be extreme fear in Bruce. I saw it, and those scamming doctors saw it also.

I informed Bruce that I needed to speak with him privately. I stated to Bruce that I no longer trusted these doctors, and that maybe the Star loans should be terminated. Bruce then suggested that instead of terminating the loans, any future withdrawals from the Star Beverage loan would require two signatures. Bruce stated that the reason he did not want to terminate the loans was because termination would prevent the company from fulfilling the $69,000,000 beverage contract with the US Navy. This comment by Stevens would later confirm that little or no due diligence had been performed by the bank on the navy contract. Bruce stated that he was sure the profits from the contract would quickly eliminate the present loan problems and requested that I continue to work with Boyd and Perry.

When the meeting with Boyd and Perry resumed, Bruce made his two-signature recommendation, and Boyd and Perry both approved of the plan. For any Star Beverage financial transaction through FirstMerit Bank, the signatures of Larry D. Jones and Arthur Boyd Jr. would be required. Boyd and Perry knew that they had achieved much more than what they had thought was possible because Bruce had just granted them a legitimate way to continue to scam FirstMerit, Erie Shores Computer, and me.

Even though the bank had instituted the two-signature requirement, Boyd knew that this requirement would not deter their plans to get the funds from the real Star account. I had warned Bruce at least twice between April and August of 2000 about trusting Boyd and Perry. During that six-month period, Boyd was able to remove the balance of the loan from the Delaware Star Beverage account in two ways: (a) by having funds removed from the account via legitimate checks that I had signed for Star business transactions. The problem with this process was that Boyd and Perry were only transferring the Star Delaware funds to Boyd's Star Beverage of Ohio account, which had a totally different federal ID number. (b) Bank records later showed that Boyd had been bold enough to forge my signature on Star Beverage checks on several occasions. Even after the FirstMerit executives became aware of these illegal activities, these executives took no actions nor did they alert me to the actions of Boyd.

What I was not aware of until years later was how, on a regular basis, Boyd and Perry threatened and intimidated Bruce and other FirstMerit executives to the point that I became the scapegoat for the bank in the loan process. The FirstMerit president and legal counsel had determined that Bruce had made critical errors while processing the Star Beverage Delaware loans. Therefore, the bank executives and their lawyers decided that it would be better for the bank if Erie Shores fought these two African American doctors, while they viewed from the sidelines. The FirstMerit executives had never experienced an assault on their bank by an African American before—not just any African American but a sociopathic African American medical doctor!

Two final bold and unthinkable actions taken by Dr. Boyd Jr. were when he showed up at the FirstMerit Bank's annual stockholder's meeting and disrupted the meeting numerous times. You must remember, I had served with these all-white bank executives and board members and knew of their inability to understand or communicate with African Americans, and Dr. Boyd, being the sociopath that he was, used fear tactics to frightened and overwhelm these bank executives. The second action of Dr. Boyd Jr. was to establish a picket in front of one of the FirstMerit Bank buildings in downtown Cleveland. The media immediately covered the picket. When the *Call & Post*, the black newspaper, picked up the story, the FirstMerit corporate board and executives and their legal team decided that Dr. Boyd was damaging the bank's image at a time when critical inroads were being made into the African American and Hispanic communities in Northern Ohio. This was when FirstMerit Bank decided it would be better for the bank if they did not fight Dr. Boyd Jr. but, instead, left Erie Shores and me personally to defend and fight a battle that should have been the bank's battle to lead and fight.

⚔️

In August 2000, after Boyd and Perry had used all of the funds in the Delaware Star account, these sociopaths had the nerve to contact me and suggest that we request the bank release the additional $400,000 loan that had been approved for Star Beverage, Delaware. I guess it was a blessing that this conversation took place over the phone and not in person because I am sure physical violence would have erupted. I told both men that they were crazy as hell if they thought Barbara and I would agree to sign for the dispersing of this second loan.

After this brief conversation was over, I placed an immediate call to Bruce and alerted him about the doctor's request and plan. Bruce never informed me that he and others at the bank had been in regular communication with the doctors. I informed Bruce that neither I nor my wife would sign the additional loan for the Delaware Star Beverage. I told Bruce again that FirstMerit should file charges against Boyd and Perry for loan fraud. Bruce's response to me was, "Larry, if I file fraud charges against Boyd and Perry, I would have to file those charges against you and Barbara."

My response was, "I don't care; go ahead and file the charges."

I was still thinking that FirstMerit, Erie Shores, and I had been scammed, and we would work together to bring Boyd, Perry, and Star Beverage down. After all, I was still a member of the FirstMerit board of directors.

We all knew that the end was coming very soon because approximately thirty days later, (September 30, 2000), the loan payment would come due. In or around mid-September, I received a call from Bruce informing me that FirstMerit had decided to grant Star Beverage a three-month loan extension. Bruce could tell by my voice that I was not pleased at FirstMerit's actions—actions that would only prolong the major fraud problem that glared brightly in front of us. Again, Bruce reminded me of the reputation I had established and the successful technology firm I had built during the prior fifteen years, and that he did not want to see all of that destroyed.

CHAPTER FORTY TWO

Again, I made a strategic mistake. I agreed to sign the loan extension agreement but not before calling Boyd and informing him and Perry that I was demanding that they replace all of the funds that they had taken from the $1.6 million bank loan. I would not have made this threat if I had known about the mind of the sociopath.

Approximately two months after the loan extension was signed, Boyd submitted a document to the Elyria police and the Federal Bureau of Investigation, stating that Bruce Stevens and I had defrauded Boyd, Perry, and Star Beverage out of the $1.6 million loan proceeds provided by FirstMerit Bank. Within a few days after Boyd sent his letter, Perry sent an almost identical letter to these same two law-enforcement agencies.

I would not become aware of these letters until approximately nine months later. This was also the first time I would become aware that Erie Shores and I were being investigated by the Federal Bureau of Investigation. During the nine months while I was unaware that

I was being investigated, Boyd, Perry, and FirstMerit Bank were in regular contact with the FBI.

After Barbara and I signed the three-month loan extension on September 30, 2000, Bruce and FirstMerit Bank eliminated all communication with me. My phone calls to Bruce at FirstMerit between October 2000 and December 31, 2000 went unanswered.

In January 2001, I had become very concerned because Bruce had not returned my calls. At that time I had no idea that Bruce was no longer employed by FirstMerit. It was not until mid-February 2001 that I was informed that Bruce Stevens was no longer employed by FirstMerit Bank. No reason for his departure was given, but I was sure it had everything to do with the Star Beverage Delaware loans.

In late January, I received a letter from Michael Milchen, Bruce's assistant, informing me of something that I already knew: the Star Beverage loan was now in default. Immediately upon receiving this notice, I made another tactical mistake by responding to Milchen's letter and informing him that I was willing to accept full responsibility for the Star loan. I continued to be sure that FirstMerit, Erie Shores, and I would fight Boyd, Perry, and Star together, but what was unknown to me at that time was that FirstMerit had already put distance between itself and Erie Shores and me.

In or around August and after numerous meetings with the FirstMerit executives and without any actions or filings against Boyd, Perry, and Star Beverage by FirstMerit Bank, I proceeded to file charges in civil court against Boyd, Perry, and Star Beverage. In September 2001, after Barbara and I agreed to assume responsibility for this $1,600,000 loan, the Lorain County Common Pleas Court awarded Erie Shores and me a judgment against Boyd, Perry, and

Star Beverage in the amount of $1,423,352.64, plus interest of 10 percent per annum, beginning on October 30, 2001.

Needless to say, I was elated to receive this major judgment. I had plans to collect on the judgment and pay off the former Star Beverage loan that Barbara and I now owned.

I would later learn that FirstMerit and its legal counsel were well aware, as early as July of 2000, that Boyd, Perry, and Star Beverage had no assets. Therefore, when Barbara and I agreed in September 2001, approximately fifteen months later, to accept the Star Beverage loan responsibility, FirstMerit executives had known for fifteen months that I would have no success in collecting any funds from the judgment against Boyd, Perry, and Star Beverage. There were no assets to collect.

By the time I became aware that I was being investigated by the Federal Bureau of Investigation, the investigation was in full force, and the providers of information against me were Boyd and Perry and possibly FirstMerit Bank.

I would later learn that Gregory White, the Lorain County prosecutor, the same prosecutor who had promised that he was "going to get me" in 1987, was closely providing assistance in the investigation against Erie Shores and me personally.

CHAPTER FORTY THREE

Richard Buie wasn't satisfied with the scams that he, Boyd, and Perry were performing on Erie Shores and my family, so he decided to introduce another friend and business associate in order to reap more financial rewards from Erie Shores. Marty Conn was the name he went by, but his real name was Marvin Cohen, an Italian Jew who appeared to be in his seventies.

I'm sure by now you are asking the question; why had I not caught on to Richard Buie and his schemes. Well, all you need to remember is, I was dealing with an associate who had a photographic memory and years to perfect his schemes on businesspersons and private citizens, including women. He was an expert, one of the best at his trade. Buie will probably cease his trade as he takes his last breath of life.

Because of Richard Buie's scams with Boyd and Perry and the debt owed by the Cuyahoga County Recorder's office, Erie Shores

Computer was now in a financial bind. I had made Buie aware of the financial strain on Erie Shores, so Buie informed me that he had a "sure" way for Erie Shores Computer to resolve its financial problems and, at the same time, establish business relationships and possibly partnerships with some powerful Cleveland Jewish businessmen.

Richard Buie and I traveled to an office building (23250 Chagrin Blvd, Beachwood, Ohio), where we met Conn in his office. Conn professed to be a successful businessman and identified several of the very visible Cleveland area Jewish businessmen as his close friends and business partners. Conn also stated that he was part owner of an AM radio station. I was not convinced that these Jewish associates were real, until I was introduced to a couple of them.

Because of this relationship with Buie and Conn, Erie Shores Computer and my family lost approximately $1.3 million in scams that were introduced as business opportunities. I can remember a couple of times when I wanted to question some of Conn's explanations about his ventures, but Buie assured me he would have Conn explain. Buie would later alert me that Conn was associated with the Jewish mafia, and that he thought I needed to know to whom I would be talking.

Shortly after Buie alerted me to Marty Conn's connections and power in Northern Ohio, an incident occurred that pretty much convinced me that Conn did indeed have this power.

CHAPTER FORTY FOUR

In mid 2000, Erie Shores Computer won and was awarded another major computer contract with the city of Cleveland, Ohio. The mayor of Cleveland at the time was Michael White. Also, by this time it had become very clear to me that Dr. Boyd and Dr. Perry had operated a scam on FirstMerit Bank, me, and Erie Shores Computer.

While this scam against Erie Shores was ongoing, Erie Shores successfully completed the delivery of products and services on the city of Cleveland contract. Instead of the city paying Erie Shores within the thirty-day period stated in the agreement, for some unknown reason, the city was delaying payment. I complained over and over for approximately seven months about this nonpayment but my complaints fell on deaf ears. This was when I decided to try the connections and power that Buie had stated Marty Conn possessed. Marty had bragged about his close relationship with Mayor Michael White and other politicians, so I figured this was a good time for him to provide proof of this relationship.

A few years later, I would become aware of two critical facts that could have caused the delay of these payments to Erie Shores: (a) Officials in the Federal Bureau of Investigation were investigating Mayor Michael White and had assumed that Erie Shores Computer had received its contract with the assistance of the mayor and his team; (b) An attorney, Michael Ryan, working full time for the city of Cleveland, was also moonlighting for Dr. Arthur Boyd and Star Beverage. I contend that both of the activities listed are possible reasons for the eight-month delay in more than $1.2 million in payment to Erie Shores Computer.

Buie arranged a meeting for me with Marty Conn, and I explained the problem I was having receiving a large payment for computers Erie Shores had delivered to the city of Cleveland. What happened next was truly amazing.

Marty Conn called Mayor White, and within two days he informed Buie that we (he, Buie, and I) had a scheduled meeting with the city of Cleveland's director of finance. A couple of days later, the three of us met with the finance director and a couple of his staff in the director's meeting room.

Marty Conn stated to the director that he did not appreciate the way Erie Shores Computer had been treated. He even used a couple of curse words while addressing the director. Conn was seated at one end of the table, and the director was seated at the opposite end. It became very clear that this was Marty Conn's meeting, and he was in total control. I had to assume that this power and authority could only have come because of Conn's close relationship with the mayor.

The director attempted to explain that Erie Shores was only one of many firms that were not being paid due to a lack of funds. Marty

Conn responded by stating that he "didn't give a damn about the other firms not being paid," but he wanted Erie Shores to begin receiving its payments immediately.

The director's response was, "I will address this immediately, Mr. Conn." This meeting came to an immediate close.

I could not believe what I had experienced during this meeting with the director of finance for the city of Cleveland. Marty Conn had just demanded and had been granted payment of more than one million dollars to Erie Shores for contract work that had been owed for more than eight months. These payments to Erie Shores Computer were to be paid biweekly, until the total amount owed was paid.

I had just experienced some of the power Marty Conn had in Northern Ohio. I was elated that Erie Shores would began to receive its money from the city of Cleveland. I was also aware that I now owed Marty Conn.

Conn knew how much I appreciated what he had done for Erie Shores, but I had no idea what this assistance would cost Erie Shores and me personally over the following thirteen months.

Marty Conn decided that Richard Buie would be the person to pick up the Erie Shores Computer checks biweekly. Logic told me that this was so that he and Buie could keep control of the payments made to Erie Shores by the city. After the first payment was delivered by Buie, Conn began to have financial needs that he expected Erie Shores to assist in covering.

The funds Erie Shores provided were actually being divided between Conn and Buie. After approximately ten weeks of payments, Buie and Conn met with me and presented what they called two great investment opportunities that needed financing. Conn and Buie were responsible for Erie Shores receiving payments from the city of Cleveland, so it was all but impossible for me to refuse to invest in the opportunities that Conn was presenting. Little did I know that both investments were scams, and that these scams were avenues for Conn and Buie to scam even larger amounts of funds from Erie Shores.

⇥⇤

What became very clear to me later was that once sociopaths become involved in your business, it is all but impossible to disconnect from them because of the tangled webs they intentionally weave. I guess Buie found his evil deeds against me and Erie Shores so easy while working with Drs. Boyd and Perry, and then with Marty Conn, that he decided to set up a venture of his own.

Even though I was sure Boyd and Perry had used Star Beverage to scam Erie Shores and FirstMerit Bank, there was nothing remotely in my mind to make me even think that Buie had been the master artist of the Star Beverage scam. Therefore, when he approached me and suggested that we (he, Conn, and I) start our own beverages firm, I wanted to know more. With the experience I had gained while working to make Star Beverage a success, I was sure that we could build a successful firm. This opportunity interested me also because Erie Shores was now bleeding cash as a result because of the scams by Star Beverages, Boyd, and Perry and the other investments Buie and Conn had involved Erie Shores in.

My trust in Richard Buie was now stronger than ever. If it had not been so strong, I would:

1. Not have invested more than one million dollars of Erie Shores Computer Inc. funds in New World Beverages LLC.

2. Not have had my sister invest more than one million in New World Beverages LLC.

3. Not have convinced my wife that we should invest more than $500,000 of our personal funds in New World Beverages LLC.

4. Have performed more due diligence before these investments and maybe uncovered the fact that Richard Buie had already incorporated a firm called New World Beverages Inc in Ohio and in Florida, prior to the incorporating of New World Beverages LLC.

5. Have known that these funds that were for investing in the growth of New World Beverages LLC were being diverted from the firm by Richard Buie and Marty Conn for their personal use.

A seriously flawed, blind trust prevented me from seeing and feeling the dark evil in Buie and Conn's actions, while I was attempting to partner and achieve success for us all. The $1,300,000 total is a conservative estimate of the total amount Buie and Conn scammed from Erie Shores, my sister, and Barbara and me.

What I would later realize was the fact that, even if New World Beverages LLC had fulfilled its beverage contracts, the New World Beverage firm that Richard Buie had secretly created would have destroyed any opportunities for long-term success.

⊷⊶

The following will give you an extremely clear picture of just how bold, traitorous, and devastating Richard Buie and Marty Conn were to my family and my company:

I contend that Buie and Conn used my personal credit rating and Erie Shores Computer's credit rating to purchase or lease products and services and obtain substantial loans from: Sears; Bank of America; BP; Capital One; US Financial Services; Toyota Motors; FirstMerit Bank; Chrysler Motors; and Key Bank.

Buie also illegally established a branch of Erie Shores Computer in Toledo, Ohio, and in Beachwood, Ohio. The tens of thousands of dollars that he secured, using my personal credit and Erie Shores' credit, were in addition to the funds scammed through his and Conn's phony investment opportunities.

CHAPTER FORTY FIVE

I n early May 2001, after two years of saying no to National City
Bank and its offer to provide more and better financing than
Huntington National Bank was providing Erie Shores, I decided to
begin discussions with National City Bank. After my outside account-
ing firm approved, I accepted National City's loan offer. The Erie
Shores headquarters building was directly across from the National
City branch. Howard Walters was the branch manager and per-
son leading the charge to convince Erie Shores to transfer its busi-
ness loan from Huntington National Bank to National City Bank.
Walters made it very clear that Erie Shores would be the only African-
American-owned firm in Lorain County to receive a business loan
from National City Bank.

National City Bank's loan agreement would eliminate the "Asset-
Based Lending" restrictions present under the Huntington National
Bank loan agreement. Additionally, the National City loan agreement increased the Erie Shores Computer line of credit from $2.5
million to $4 million.

The Erie Shores line of credit with National City Bank was signed on July 6, 2001. Only God knew what was in store for the United States and the world approximately sixty-five days later. September 11, 2001 is a day that will live in infamy. America had only been attacked once before on its soil, by an enemy—an enemy that used the equipment and assets of Americans to carry out the brazen attack on the World Trade Towers of New York City and the US Pentagon in Washington, DC.

I could not believe what I was viewing on my office TV, when I actually watched in real time as the second airplane crashed into the second World Trade Tower. Time stood still for a few minutes that day. When time resumed, I tried to process what had just happened. A few hours later, I had become aware that hundreds of American lives had just been lost, and that two of the World Trade Towers had been totally destroyed. The next day I would also realize that some country and its people would pay an extremely heavy price for this unprovoked attack on the United States of America.

I also knew the United States and the world would never be the same. What I did not realize at the time was the heavy price Erie Shores, my family, and I would have to pay because of this tragedy.

The attack had killed more than two thousand and had injured hundreds more. The United States ceased all flights within the country, and the US economy was devastated for more than eighteen months. Banks and other financial institutions ceased to make loans for months, and those businesses that had loans saw many additional restrictions put in place on those loans. Erie Shores had not had time to use its new line of credit that it had just received sixty-five days earlier.

Without any notice by Howard Walters or any other National City Bank official, Erie Shores' $4 million line of credit saw new and more stringent rules put in place. This meant that Erie Shores could only borrow the amount of funds that it had sales to cover, which were the same rules that Erie Shores had under its former Huntington National Bank line of credit.

A large percentage of Erie Shores' sales were to state and federal governmental agencies and educational agencies; therefore, when National City decided to eliminate these sales from the approved sales for the $4 million line of credit, Erie Shores was left with a non-usable $4 million line of credit. In addition to these exclusions, National City Bank refused to provide Erie Shores Computer any working capital along with this $4 million line of credit, thus rendering this line of credit all but useless to Erie Shores. This was the loan that later became known as the "nigger loan" because these type loans from National City were reserved for black and Hispanic individuals and businesses in Northern Ohio.

The attack on the United States had pretty much forced the local, state, and federal governments to drastically reduce the awarding of contracts and to cancel many others. Erie Shores suffered more than the average firm because more than 60 percent of its sales were to the government and educational institutions.

Erie Shores had lost a large percentage of its state and federal business. Also, because of the restrictions and changes National City Bank had made to Erie Shores' line of credit and because National City had not provided any working capital to cover monthly operating expenses, business activity continued to decline.

CHAPTER FORTY SIX

This was when, during an eight-month period, I made the decision that if I was going to keep Erie Shores afloat, I would be required to take drastic measures. I was positive that those federal contracts that Erie Shores had in-house would not be cancelled; but a larger number of them were cancelled. These cancellations left me with no funds to pay overhead expenses and salaries.

I decided to make funds available to Erie Shores from its $4 million line of credit by breaking a couple of the National City Bank's loan rules that had been changed after the 9/11 attacks. Not having working capital to cover these expenses, I decided to take the drastic, but temporary, step of increasing some of the Erie Shores' customer sales invoices in order to be able to use the $4 million line of credit. I projected that Erie Shores' sales would surely rebound within a three- to four-month period, in time for me to replace the funds that would be used to cover operating expenses. I knew that I had to replace these funds prior to the biannual bank audit that was approximately fifteen months away.

The September 11, 2011 horrors had struck more of a devastating blow to the private and public economy than anyone, even the most learned economists, had predicted. Three months had now passed since I had begun increasing customer invoices. I continued to remain pretty calm about my actions because I had more than one "ram in the bush."

I was quite sure that Erie Shores' sales would return to normal within a few months. I had also been promised and assured an infusion of funds for Erie Shores and New World Beverages by Marty Conn from his Jewish friends. With sales returning to normal and this infusion of cash, Erie Shores would have more than enough funds to cover the funds I had used to cover the Erie Shores operating expenses. More than five months passed, and no increase in sales had occurred. I was also now seriously concerned about the investments from these Jewish friends of Marty Conn (Marvin Cohen). Of course, Conn and Buie always had convincing and logical reasons for the investment delays.

At this point, I figured I had three logical choices: (a) report my loan activities to National City Bank and suffer the consequences, (b) continue to pursue the $1.4 million outstanding judgment against Boyd, Perry, and Star Beverage, hoping against hope that we would locate some of their hidden funds, or (c) continue to increase the sales invoices in order to cover the Erie Shores operating expenses and continue to hope and pray that sales would increase really soon and that these friends of Conn would make good on their funding promises.

Well, to make a long story shorter, I continued to increase the Erie Shores sales invoices, but the sales did not increase substantially, and Conn's friends never came through on their funding promises. It would become very clear later that these Jewish "friends" of Conn had no knowledge that he and Buie had used their names to promote scams against Erie Shores and my family.

CHAPTER FORTY SEVEN

I will highlight Dr. Arthur Boyd and the evils of him and Richard Buie. As I search for solace and comfort, it comes only in knowing that I somehow, mentally and physically, survived five of the most evil sociopaths with which anyone could ever associate. I now have factual evidence that evil spirits exists, and the evil ones always come to cause harm, fear, confusion, mistrust, destruction, and even death.

＝━╬ ╬━＝

It think it is important that my readers get a clear understanding of the low level of ethics and morals of the professional people who had invaded my life. The information below lists the activities of the second most dangerous sociopath. Richard Buie holds the number-one position, and he is the one who opened the portal that three of the other sociopaths entered through.

The following timeline of Arthur Boyd Jr. will paint a clear picture of this person and his activities.

1947	Born in Durham, North Carolina.
1969	Earns bachelor's degree from Florida A& M.
1978	Graduates Meharry Medical School, Nashville, Tennessee.
1978	Boyd takes his first Federation of State Medical Boards licensing exam (FLEX) and fails. In all, he will fail this test fifteen times between 1978 and 1995.
1978-1980	Intern at Howard University Hospital, Washington, DC. Claims to have trained under prominent surgeon Debakey in that same time period.
1981-1984	Resident in surgery, St Luke's Hospital, Cleveland, Ohio. Leaves shortly after he and hospital are sued for medical malpractice.
1984	Fails another FLEX test exam.
1984	Offers $20,000 to Michigan state official for advance copy of next FLEX exam. Arrested and convicted of attempted bribery.
1984-1985	Allegedly worked as a Fellow in prestigious University of Pittsburgh Liver Transplant Program. Official report states that he just "hung out" there.
1985	Pleads no contest in Michigan bribery case. Then appeals. Judgment affirmed. Serves his time in 1987.

1986	Incorporates Motown Beverage; operates it as Town Club.
1988	Lists himself in Who's Who as "Chief Surgeon" Motown Beverage Corporation. When inquired, could not explain why a beverage firm needed a chief surgeon.
1988	Denied medical license in Ohio for felony conviction.
1988	Denied medical license in Alaska for falsification of license application.
1988	Denied medical license in Connecticut for felony conviction.

Late 1980s Practiced medicine in the Caribbean

1992	Asked Ohio court to seal records of his criminal conviction from licensing authorities, potential employers, and general public.
1993	Denied medical license in California for falsification of application and felony conviction.
1993	Secures position at Maryland Shock Trauma Center by falsifying employment application. Performs at least 125 unlicensed surgeries.
1994	Secures right to sell pop to the navy. Misrepresents to investors, banks, and others over the following ten years, using a bogus beverage contract stated to be worth $69 million. Scammed millions of dollars using this bogus contract.

1995   Exposed by the *Baltimore Sun* newspaper for performing surgeries at the Maryland Shock Trauma Center without a license. Discharged from employment. Sues hospital and *Baltimore Sun* in federal court for libel. First of barrage of frivolous lawsuits filed by Boyd. Trauma Center appears to have dropped federal suit because Boyd had officially requested the names and addresses of all of the patients he had illegally performed surgery on because he wanted to send them letters of apology.

1996   Sued by Motown Records in federal court in New York for incorporating his beverage firm, Motown Beverage. This was done in an attempt to capitalize on goodwill of the Motown name.

1997   Denied medical license in state of Washington for attempting to obtain license by misrepresentation.

1997   Motown Records obtains injunction against Boyd.

1998   Federal Court of Appeals affirms Motown Records judgment.

1998   Boyd sues Pennsylvania medical licensing board for refusing to permit him to take the FLEX test. Dismissed on summary judgment.

1998   Boyd and Perry form Star Beverage Corporation of Delaware.

1998   Boyd sues Motown lawyer Ken Bressler for $43 million in federal court in Cleveland, Ohio, for disclosing his conviction in court filings. Case later dismissed on summary judgment and affirmed by Federal Court of Appeals.

1999   Sues Ohio State Medical Board for disclosing his conviction to Attorney Bressler. Case dismissed on summary judgment and affirmed on appeal.

2001   Motown Records wins sanctions judgment against Boyd for $119,715.39 for violating federal court injunction, filing baseless motions in court, and attempting to relitigate matters already decided.

2002   Federal Court of Appeals upholds Motown sanctions against Boyd but reduces award to $80,000. Boyd never paid this debt or any other debts ordered by state or federal courts.

Over a twelve year period Dr. Arthur Boyd Jr. scammed substantial amounts of funds from the following persons:

1. Mr. Lemar Frost; Cleveland, Ohio
2. Mr. James McBride; Cleveland, Ohio
3. Dr. Chester Wilson; Canton, Ohio
4. Mr. Raymond Singletary; Akron, Ohio
5. Ms. Debbie Calloway; Cleveland, Ohio
6. Dr. Michelle Spain; Cleveland, Ohio
7. Mr. Robert Vaughn; Shaker Heights, Ohio
8. Mr. Fred Finley; Cleveland, Ohio
9. Mr. Mark Cocroft; Detroit, Michigan
10. Ms. Gwen Valerie; Detroit Michigan
11. Mr. Cleveland Brown; Norfolk, Virginia

Note: The names of persons listed above were included in my sworn affidavit sent to US Attorney, Gregory White on December 3, 2003.

Questions that I had after becoming aware of Boyd's activities were:

1. How could the executives of FirstMerit Regional Bank, after due diligence, approve a $1.6 million and $400,000 loan to this guy as one of the owners of Star Beverage?

2. After all of Dr. Boyd's activities in state and federal courts, why would the FBI investigate the March 2000 $2 million Star Beverage loan scam at FirstMerit Bank in Elyria, Ohio, for four years and make no arrest but later used/misuse that information to arrest me for the misuse of Erie Shores' line of credit at National City Bank?

3. Why has the FBI permitted Arthur Boyd Jr. to continue committing fraud and scamming people?

4. Why did the FBI permit criminal charges to be dropped against Boyd in 1995, after he had performed more than 125 unlicensed surgeries at the Maryland Trauma Center?

⟨⟩

Dr. Merceda Perry—what a mess. Perry had his doctor's office and his Star Beverage office in the same building, occupying the same space in Greensboro, North Carolina. My hiring of the North Carolina law firm of Smith, Helms, Mullis & Moore and their investigation of Dr. Merceda Perry uncovered some interesting information:

1. Merceda Perry was married to Willia Perry and lived most of the time with his wife in Asheboro, North Carolina.

2. The property he owned in Asheboro had five liens attached, liens FirstMerit Bank should have discovered when performing its due diligence prior to the loan to Star Beverage Delaware.

3. Perry had ownership in four firms in addition to Star Beverage and his physician practice: Nutra Science (William Hunter), Greensboro; Delta Group (Raymond Brown), Asheboro; Granite Industries (Art Enoch), Rockwell; and Quinn Specialty (John Quinn), Dunn, North Carolina.

4. Even though Perry had five liens on his home property, he had part ownership in these additional firms and also had enough extra funds to purchase for his mistress, Lynette, who lived in Charlotte, North Carolina, an $80,000 Mercedes.

5. **A portion of number five is speculation based on facts:** I only met Steve McIver, Perry's office manager twice, although we had numerous phone conversations. Steve was approximately twenty-two years old. He was so attractive he could have been considered pretty and could easily have been a model. When Steve picked me up at the Raleigh/Durham Airport, during our ride to Greensboro, he informed me that his fiancee was in med school at the University of North Carolina. Right away I knew something was very odd about Steve working as Perry's office manager. Dr. Perry was an overweight, verb-splitting individual who somehow had completed his medical degree. The few times Perry had spoken of Steve, very little respect was shown. The investigation of Smith, Helm, Mullis & Moore uncovered the fact that Dr. Perry was not a person of high ethics and morals. During my last phone conversation with Steve, I asked him why, with his looks and such a brilliant mind, was he working as Perry's office manager. His response lead me to believe that he was being blackmailed by Dr. Perry. All indications were that Perry was molesting Steve and had threatened to out him as being homosexual if he did not continue as his office manager. Steve

appeared to be deeply in love with his fiancee and knew that he would lose her if what Perry was doing to him was ever revealed. Only Steve knows the truth about why he was working an extremely low paying job that he hated, for a person who had little to no respect for him.

6. The final information that I shared with FBI Special Agent David Lyons was the fact that Perry had died of a massive heart attack in June 2002. I am quite sure many were pleased to hear this news, but no one more pleased than Steve. **End of speculation based on facts.**

CHAPTER FORTY EIGHT

I have always believed strongly that African Americans and Hispanics in Northern Ohio, and especially Lorain County, were being left out of the opportunities of business ownership and management. Therefore, from the time I served as a sales engineer with US Steel Corporation, I would highlight these problems and the importance of inclusion. After working successfully to bring an Urban League chapter to Lorain County and agreeing to serve as its first chairman, I was given the platform and opportunity to address these problems from a much broader base. Speaking as board chairman of the league, I assumed that the community would view me as speaking for and through the league, but that was not the case.

My ideals and visions as the chairman of league were instituted and used also as a guide for how I operated Erie Shores Computer. This was why the thirty-four Erie Shores employees were the most diverse in Lorain County. This was also the reason I used the services of African American and Hispanic firms whenever possible, including the legal services of Michael Ross, one of only two African American attorneys in Lorain County.

⊷⊶

In or around 1993, I had heard about this young black man who had returned to Lorain County from New York City to attend the funeral of his mother. After the funeral he decided to remain in the county. Michael Ross had political aspirations. When I met him, he had already made an unsuccessful run for a county-wide seat as a Lorain County commissioner.

In or around 1994, I had the opportunity to meet Ross while we both served on the Lorain County Community Action Agency's board of directors. From what I could tell, Ross had become a leader in the Lorain City community. At the time I wasn't familiar with the City of Lorain but wanted to become more familiar because of my position with the league. I would quickly become aware of the divide between the cities of Elyria and Lorain. This divide was not only in the African American and Hispanic communities; the divide was well established in the white communities also, including the business and civic communities. Because my position with US Steel required me to devote most of my time outside of Lorain County, at the expense of spending time with my family, I devoted my other hours involved in community projects, sponsored by the league.

It would take almost fifteen years of diplomacy and effective communication before the two cities (Elyria and Lorain) would begin to work together as part of a region. Because of my activities as chairman of the Lorain County Urban League, I was able to work with both cities, their business communities, and, with extra effort, the NAACP chapters and El Centro. Because of the league's activities, I was able to work somewhat effectively with the politicians in the two cities and throughout Lorain County.

⊷ ⊶

In 1996 Michael Ross approached me and informed me that was planning to run again for a Lorain County commissioner's seat. He informed me that his win would be historical because no African American had ever been elected to a county-wide political position.

At the time I had become the first African American to serve on a bank's board of directors in the county and also the first to become a member of one of the two, local country clubs, Spring Valley Country Club.

I knew very little about Michael Ross, only what I had heard, and what I had heard impressed me. I thought that it would be great for the Urban League and the county if Ross could become a county commissioner. I knew one of Ross's problems would be raising enough funds to run an effective campaign. I also knew that I was the only African American in the county in a position to sponsor an affair in an environment where the entire community would feel welcome or, at the least, impressed. I knew Ross would make this fund-raising request, and he did. After his request, I agreed to hold a fund-raiser for him at Spring Valley Country Club.

A very successful fund-raiser was held, and there were more than three hundred people in attendance. I was extremely pleased at the number of white citizens in attendance. Little did I know the profound effect this fund-raiser would have on my future. From that fund-raiser forward, all of the movers and shakers as well as the average citizens—black, Hispanic, and white—in Lorain County made various assumptions about me: (1) because I was a member of the

Spring Valley Country Club, (2) because I was holding a fund-raiser for Ross, we must be close friends, (3) because I was a member of the country club, many of the African Americans attending the function became jealous of my country club membership. The most devastating thing that happened that evening occurred because I had sponsored such a highly visible county-wide political function. Became of this function, I became an even larger target for Lorain County prosecutor, Gregory White, and many of his Republican friends.

I was unaware that people had perceived Ross and I as close friends, and my extremely busy schedule—building Erie Shores Computer; serving on the Premier Bank board of directors, St Joseph Hospital's board of trustees, and the boards of The United Way, Community Foundation, Lorain County 20/20, African American Fund, Lorain County Board of Mental Health, Lorain County Community Action Agency, Greater Cleveland Growth Association's Minority Input Committee, and the Lorain County Urban League—limited the development of any kind of close business or personal relationships or friendships.

I would later realize that this perceived close friendship between Michael Ross and me had become an assumed fact in Lorain County. Because I did not get to know Ross, I was unaware of his prior sociopathic behavior and actions. All I saw was a bright, intelligent young African American with a law degree from Case Western Reserve University, who was reaching beyond the norm to become the first African American to hold a county-wide elected office.

Many of the leaders in the African American and Hispanic communities were aware of Michael Ross and his history of questionable and possibly illegal activities, but not one of them warned me about the possible dangers a perceived close relationship or friendship with Michael Ross could bring.

I felt it was a great day in Lorain County when Ross won his county-wide commissioner's seat. Ross's credibility in the white community had come as a result of his serving as the Safety Service Director in the city of Lorain for three years. His credibility in the Hispanic community was because of the relationships he had developed with various leaders. His support in the African American community came because he was one of only two African American attorneys and the first Black to seek and be elected to a county-wide office.

I made Ross aware of the long running battles I had experienced against Prosecutor, Gregory White and the funds that the commissioners had awarded Erie Shores Computer in 1987. I informed Ross that White and I had been adversaries for years.

Ross shared with me that during his three years while serving as Safety Service Director in the city of Lorain, he had numerous negative encounters with Prosecutor White and considered him to be a closet racist who used his office to discriminate against African Americans and Hispanic/Latinos on a regular basis.

I relayed to Ross that my only two requests for providing assistance in his victory were; (a) make sure the county hired additional African Americans and Hispanics, and (b) that the county start providing support to the minority businesses in the county. At the time Ross was sworn in, there were only three African American county employees. Minority business participation in county contracts was pretty much nonexistent and not a concern of the three Democratic county commissioners. Erie Shores had not participated in a county contract since 1986 (the contract that was contested by Erie Shores), and now the year was 1997. Ross promised me he would work to see that improvements were made in both areas.

After approximately six months in office, it was becoming clear that Ross was not paying enough attention to his duties as county commissioner. Even though the county had increased its hiring of minorities, he was seldom present for meetings and spent a great deal of his time outside of the county and the state. Because of his level of intelligence, coupled with his sociopathic thought process, Ross, even though he seldom attended the commissioner's meetings, was able to convince the two female county commissioners to pass legislation that he recommended on a regular basis.

Hindsight led me to believe that many persons in the business, civic, and African American and Hispanic communities knew about Ross's dark side. One of my white attorneys was aware that Ross had represented his (Ross) mother-in-law in a vehicle accident, and she had been awarded a substantial sum of money. Instead of his mother-in-law receiving the majority of these funds, Ross was supposed to have used most of those funds for his personal benefit.

It appears that this kind of action was pretty much the norm for Ross, but no one publicized these actions by Ross, not until I had been caught up in one of Ross's schemes. After it was too late, many persons came forth to warn me about Ross. A number of the black leaders commented to me, "Mr. Jones, I knew Ross was a bad seed; he came from bad stock." At this point, their comments only pissed me off because I knew they were not sharing this information for the purpose of helping me.

⊷╬╫⊶

The two African American lawyers in Lorain County, Ross and a female name Freddie Springfield, were totally different. Ross was outgoing, bold, and at times brazen. Attorney Springfield was very bright but lacked aggressiveness and showed little self-confidence.

My greatest disappointment in my relationship with Freddie was when, after months of campaigning for her to become only the second black judge in Lorain County, she, without any explained reason, made an abrupt decision to withdraw from the race. To date, she has yet to provide a clear reason explaining her actions. At least three of us who had worked so hard on her campaign deduced that Attorney Springfield had received a call from someone representing the power base that controlled her future as a successful lawyer in Lorain County.

Ross's law firm was a one-man show but because of his status, he appeared to be well connected with the major law firms in the county. He informed me that he was working closely with the county prosecutor's office on various cases, in spite of Prosecutor White's objections. What Ross did not tell me was that the county and city officials were keeping a close eye on him because of his clientele.

My main law firm was Fauver, Tattersal & Gallagher, but when Ross approached me about getting some of the Erie Shores legal business, I felt I could not say no. After all, minority business participation was what I had been preaching in the county for more than thirteen years.

I assigned Ross a couple of small legal cases that Erie Shores had that needed attention, and I was impressed how they were handled. My biggest problem was attempting to locate or contact Ross when needed, due to his travels.

CHAPTER FORTY NINE

I was well aware, through the various media outlets, that the county was in the process of planning to erect a new Lorain County Justice Center. This project would be the largest in the history of the county. I had plans to participate as a minority subcontractor by signing up with as many prime contractors as possible. I knew Erie Shores could not be a prime contractor on such a large venture, but I was very sure that Erie Shores could participate as a subcontractor and provide some of the technology requirements.

I informed Ross of my interest in participating with firms that had planned to submit bids for the building of the Justice Center. When Ross met with me and informed me that he would work to assure Erie Shores getting opportunities to participate as a subcontractor, I was elated. Ross informed me that I needed to focus on the firms bidding for the General Manager and Architect requirements in the construction of the Justice Center. These would be the firms with which to seek attractive subcontracting relationships.

At the time, Ross was in an uphill battle to be reelected to his county commissioner's seat because of the subpar job he had done in his first four years as commissioner. Therefore, getting this massive construction project approved and the primes and subcontractors in place prior to possibly losing his power as a commissioner were of extreme importance. To assure that the two firms would be awarded the architect and general manager contracts for the Justice Center construction, Ross and his two fellow commissioners voted to replace Virgil Mauntean, the present county administrator, with James Cordes. A few weeks after this change in county administrators, the commissioners awarded the two contracts to two of the firms Erie Shores had already agreed to establish a subcontracting relationship.

⊨⊹ ⊹⊫

Ross was defeated in his bid to be reelected to his county commissioner's seat, but he had been successful in achieving what he had most wanted and needed. I would soon be informed by Ross that he was in serious financial trouble and owed a substantial sum of money to some very bad people, and that he may be in need of my assistance.

When I met Michael Ross, I took for granted that this young man was a godsend for Lorain County. He had everything together: he was handsome, intelligent, and savvy, and he presented himself extremely well.

Little did I know nor did I take the time to check his background or get to know him personally. I just assumed that he was an honest, upstanding professional African American male, and I had planned to do everything in my power to assist in his political future.

Those who knew Ross's travel schedule knew he had good reasons why he was absent from many commissioner's meetings. He was busy traveling the country with the Lorain City mayor, Alex Oleko, developing friendships with other mayors, commissioners, and business leaders.

While serving as Safety Service Director, Ross became very friendly with Mayor Alex Oleko. The mayor had total confidence in Ross. Ross used that friendship with the mayor to create his and the mayor's travel schedule. Ross was the reason he and Mayor Oleko traveled the country, attending political functions that were of very little value to the mayor and the city but extremely important to Ross. These contacts served Ross well because he was a master in the art of name dropping. He knew that just by dropping the name of one of his local, state, or national contacts, people would automatically assume that he had power. Mayor Oleko was traveling the nation, meeting dignitaries whom he would have never met on his own.

Ross knew that I was looking forward to providing computer hardware, software, and printers for the new Justice Center, so he kept me updated on the process. Ross could not meet with the potential architectural and general manager firms that he thought would be awarded the contracts; therefore, he informed me that I should meet with representatives of these firms and present Erie Shores' capabilities.

Ross provided me the names of the four top firms, and I proceeded to schedule meetings. Instead of meeting with the executive of the architectural firm that eventually won the bid, I met with a gentleman who represented the firm. This meeting went quite well. I presented Erie Shores to the representative and informed him that Erie Shores was interested in subcontracting with a prime firm in building the County Justice Center.

A few days later, I met with the presidents of two of the firms that were later ranked first and second in the running for the general manager contract.

It was a warm Monday morning when I drove to the Holiday Inn in Westlake, Ohio, to meet the president of the firm that would eventually be awarded the general manager contract. My breakfast guest spotted me right away; after all, not too many African American businessmen frequented the Westlake Holiday Inn. The two of us had breakfast while we presented our firms. At the end of the seventy-five-minute breakfast, we agreed to be in contact within a few days. This gentleman was of Italian decent, approximately six feet tall, and absent of body fat. I could tell that he was a no nonsense businessman. During half of the breakfast, I felt at times as though I was being interrogated. In parting that morning, this gentleman, while shaking my hand, looked into my eyes as though he was looking through me and commented, "Jones, I hope your firm can perform as you have stated."

Later that day I spoke via phone with Ross to update him and to let him know that the gentleman whom I had met with that morning made me feel uneasy. Ross assured me that he knew him well, and that he was a good businessman.

The three commissioners held their meeting to announce the firms that had been awarded the architectural contract and the general manager contract. The winners were two of the four firms with which Erie Shores had agreed to sign subcontract agreements.

⟞⟨⟩⟝

Ross was living fast: the travel, women, and drugs had become an addiction to him, but again, I did not see or feel this danger, mainly because we very seldom spent more than thirty to forty minutes together during our business meetings. Ross and I never met on a social basis.

What began as one of the best contractual opportunities Erie Shores had ever had in Lorain County would turn into a subcontract of lies, greed, and indirect intimidation.

Approximately one week after Erie Shores had signed the subcontracting agreement with the two firms, I received a frantic call from Ross, informing me that he needed to meet with me that evening. He directed me to meet him at the Rubin's Sandwich Shop, across State Route 57, at the Midway Mall in Elyria.

Ross had already arrived when I arrived and was waiting in his car. As he exited his vehicle, I noticed a gym bag in his hand. My first question to Ross was: Why was he carrying a gym bag? I immediately saw what I thought was fear in his face. Ross reached into the gym bag and pulled out a 38 pistol and said, "Man, I am in trouble and need this for protection."

My question to him was, "What the hell are you talking about?"

By this time we were entering the sandwich shop; the pistol had been returned to the bag. After being seated, Ross informed me that he had been trying not to come to me for assistance, but he now had no one else to turn to. He stated that he had received substantial loans from some people and had not been able to repay these loans. If he was not able to repay what he owed, he felt that his life would be pretty much over. I let Ross know immediately that I wanted no part of his problems.

Ross's response was, "Larry, I am sorry but to keep these guys off me this long, I had to tell them something, so I led them to believe that I was part owner of Erie Shores Computer."

I wanted to kick his ass right there in the sandwich shop, but I did not want to cause a scene, and I also remembered the 38 pistol in his bag. It took a few minutes for me to regain my composure, as I literally ignored Ross's sixty to ninety seconds of apologies. Ross informed me that his creditors were extremely dangerous, and if they could not get funds from him, they would probably come after Erie Shores and me personally.

Once Ross knew that I was composed enough to listen, he proceeded to inform me that he had a plan in mind that would give him the ability to repay the loans he owed these people, and his plan would not require any funds from Erie Shores nor me personally.

I just needed to permit his funds to flow through Erie Shores from the two firms that Erie Shores would be subcontracting with on the Lorain County Justice Center.

⊨⊱ ⊰⊨

It did not take much convincing for me to believe that Ross was involved with people who made these types of loans, because I had Googled one of the firms that had been awarded the Justice Center contract. What I read gave me great concern, and now Erie Shores was subcontracting with this firm. I knew Ross had made it possible for this firm to be awarded the contract and also for Erie Shores to become its subcontractor. Knowing this, I was pretty sure Ross was using both firms to achieve his goals and stay alive.

I was now beginning to realize the possible danger ahead for me, my family, and Erie Shores. For the next few days my total awake hours were spent trying to decide if it would be better for my family and me and Erie Shores if I assisted Ross with his plans or reported Ross to the Lorain County prosecutor.

After much thought and many prayers for guidance, I made the decision to assist Ross with his plan and permit his funds from the building of the County Justice Center to flow through Erie Shores.

I came to the conclusion that it would be a major mistake to go to the county prosecutor because the Lorain County prosecutor was Gregory White. It is now around 2001, and Gregory White and I had not spoken since 1987, when I threatened to sue the Lorain County commissioners.

The threat made against me by Lorain County Prosecutor White in the presence of both of my attorneys that day in 1987 convinced me that it would be a serious mistake to inform the prosecutor's office about the illegal actions being planned for the Justice Center. I was pretty sure Prosecutor White would somehow include me as a participant in the scheme and use this as the way to get back at me, as he had promised. I was also concerned about having police protection for my family if I exposed Ross's plan—protection not so much from Ross but from the people whom Ross owed the funds.

After making my decision to assist Ross in the transfer of funds to pay his debt, this was when he informed me that his total debt to these individuals was $600,000.

When the funds began to come into the Erie Shores account, some checks from the Lorain County government and some directly from the two firms, I then had checks provided to Ross from the Erie Shores account and, later, from my personal bank account. This plan was working as smoothly as Ross had promised. To cover these transfers of funds, Ross created Market Shapes, a shell company.

Erie Shores would end up not making money on the building of the Lorain County Justice Center, but I felt I had literally saved Ross's life and, at the same time, kept Erie Shores and my family from an extremely dangerous situation.

CHAPTER FIFTY

Ross informed me that he had a legal case that he was now working, and he felt his client may be interested in investing in Erie Shores or New World Beverages.

Ross wanted to bring his client, a "Young Lady" by my office after normal working hours in order for me to meet her and discuss the possibilities of her investing. I will refer to this person as "Young Lady" only because of the brutal and tragic ending to her life. She was quite attractive, and she had a great personality and a beautiful body, and she was physically fit. She appeared to be of Italian decent and in her mid-thirties. I would be in this Young Lady's presence only twice; the second time was when I accompanied Ross to pick her up from the health spa in Westlake, Ohio, a month or so later.

Ross and this Young Lady came by the office that evening, and after the introductions, she informed me that she was from St Louis, Missouri, and that she indeed had funds that she wanted to possibly invest in firms such as New World Beverages and Erie Shores Computer. Ross then let the Young Lady know that she could share with me why she was in Lorain County.

Ross had informed me a few months earlier about his father, Emmitt Ross's, bail bond company. Michael Ross used the services of his father's firm to provide the bail amount needed for this Young Lady to be released from the Lorain County Jail. Michael had agreed to serve as her legal counsel. The young lady told me she was in Lorain County because she had been arrested on numerous drug and related charges, the most serious charge being attempting to bring a massive amount of drugs into Lorain County via train. The drop-off was said to be an old box car switching station off State Route 254, close to the Elyria/Lorain borders. During our forty-minute meeting, the Young Lady never once denied her involvement in this drug activity. She seemed to be confident that Ross would be of great assistance in resolving her problems. She informed me that she was interested in investing, in New World Beverages and possibly Erie Shores Computer, and that her untainted funds were in a trust that was controlled by her and her mother.

A couple of days later, I inquired of Ross about how he planned to help this Young Lady with her charges. He first shared with me that the Young Lady had a friend whom he had met. This friend had traveled from Detroit to Elyria and presented him a brown paper bag full of cash to cover her legal expenses.

A few weeks later, I met with Ross and was informed that all of the Young Lady's legitimate funds were controlled totally by her mother. What she had failed to point out was that she and her mother had not spoken in two years, so an investment by the Young Lady would probably never happen.

Ross also informed me that he was pretty sure the Young Lady would become a witness for Lorain prosecutor, Gregory White, in the prosecution of her boss, a drug kingpin out of Youngstown, Ohio. For her testifying, charges would be dropped, and the Young Lady would receive a new identity and be relocated. Ross stated that his client had been promised this by Prosecutor White, and he would be working closely with Prosecutor Greg White to make sure that his client received what she had been promised.

Ross also stated that he had been informed about how important this major case was to Prosecutor Greg White. This was the largest drug case ever uncovered in Lorain County, and the Prosecutor knew that if he was able to get a conviction, he would receive national attention. Ross confirmed his commitment and the commitment of his client in the prosecution of the kingpin, as long as the charges against the Young Lady were dropped and she was given that new identity and relocated. Ross stated that Prosecutor White and the FBI were well aware that it would be extremely important for this Young Lady to receive a new identity and be relocated because of the known brutality of the man she was about to testify against.

━━◃┼▹━━

Ross informed me that he began to realize that he had been lied to by Prosecutor White, after receiving a call from the Young Lady, informing him that she had been assigned Dennis Will, an Elyria police officer, to protect her. Ross told her to keep him updated on all actions and conversations by this City of Elyria police officer. It did not take long for this officer to begin confiding personally in this Young Lady whom he had been assigned to protect.

The Young Lady's initial concerns were about the officer's constant personal conversations about his life. Her first confidential message to Ross was that the officer had felt comfortable enough with her to pose the question to her, "Why do you have that nigger representing you on this case?" Ross had voiced concerns about trusting Prosecutor White because he was pretty sure that he had not wanted him representing this Young Lady.

The prosecutor's plans did not work because the Young Lady was a stranger in the area and felt that she could only trust Ross, her attorney and now close friend.

Her having Ross as her attorney did not stop this officer from becoming infatuated with the Young Lady. She kept Ross updated on many of the officer's comments to her during the many weeks he provided protection for the Young Lady while in Lorain and Cuyahoga County and in the Chicago area.

The following are some of the Young Lady's comments that were left on Ross's cell phone voice mail, which she stated Detective Dennis Will had made to her. Ross permitted me to listen to some of the voice mails and some of the comments I was privy to are listed below.

A. "Michael, I think he is coming on to me."

B. "This redneck is trying to get me to fire you as my attorney. He ask me why did I have that nigger representing me, and that I should get rid of you. Michael, he is a redneck, but I can control him because I think he is infatuated with me."

C. "I think he wants to get in my panties."

D. "He is so persistent; he concerns me at times because he wants to protect me too much."

E. "Michael, he acts like he is not getting any at home. Maybe I should let him see it, smell it, and maybe lick it. What do you think? (then laughter); that should be enough to satisfy his fat ass.

A few months later, Ross informed me that he and his client had completed their agreement, and the Young Lady would testify against her kingpin boss. The Young Lady did indeed testify against her boss. He was incarcerated, and all of the charges against the Young Lady were supposedly dropped. She was also supposedly given a new identity and relocated by federal officials.

It appears that someone did not follow through with the promises made to this Young Lady because less than two years later, her badly burned body was found in the trunk of a burned-out vehicle. This vehicle was found in the Young Lady's hometown of St. Louis, Missouri.

CHAPTER FIFTY ONE

During the pretrial phases for this Young Lady, Erie Shores was experiencing two rather serious legal issues: one with Compaq Computer and the other with Microsoft Corporation. The successful way Ross appeared to be handling the criminal case led me to believe that he could handle two major civil cases that were on the horizon. Indeed, when these cases arose, instead of using my main legal firm, Fauver, Tattersal & Gallagher, I decided to use the services of Ross's firm.

Ross and I held conference calls with the legal counsels representing Compaq and Microsoft, for the purpose of introducing Ross as the Erie Shores attorney. After providing Ross all the necessary documents and updates on the specific charges of Microsoft and Compaq, he was supposed to represent and guide Erie Shores in the pretrial sessions and meetings and to brief and update me on a regular basis. I scheduled weekly Monday afternoon meetings where Ross and I would meet in my office to address the charges against Erie Shores by Compaq Computer Corporation and Microsoft Corporation.

For three Mondays Ross and I met, and for three Mondays Ross updated me on the progress he had made with the local lawyers for Compaq and Microsoft Corporation. From Ross's weekly reports, he was making great progress with both corporations and possibly getting close to a settlement with both firms.

At the end of that third Monday afternoon meeting, I informed Ross that we would need to meet again the next day (Tuesday afternoon) to discuss additional documents related to both the Compaq and Microsoft legal proceedings.

Tuesday afternoon came, and Ross did not show up for this critical meeting. Numerous calls to his cell phone on Tuesday afternoon went unanswered. On Wednesday afternoon Ross arrived at my office, wearing the same blue-striped suit that he had worn for our Monday afternoon meeting. Not only was he wearing the same suit, he had on the same shirt and tie, and his body odor confirmed that he had probably not bathed since leaving my office.

At this point I was pretty sure where Ross had been and why he was in his present condition. When he spoke and informed me that he was there for our Tuesday afternoon meeting, I knew he had a serious problem. His bloodshot eyes and the fact that he was fidgety pretty much confirmed that Ross had a drug problem. Some of the Urban League clients had spoken about a drug house in downtown Lorain, a house not far from Ross's office. The attorney whom I had put in charge of two of the most critical civil cases in the history of Erie Shores was now sitting in my office on Wednesday afternoon, thinking it was Tuesday afternoon.

I exploded on Ross. I told him that it was Wednesday and not Tuesday, and that I knew he was on drugs. I told him that he smelled like shit and looked like hell. Ross's eyes grew larger, and he quickly stood from his seat and rushed from my office, without saying a word. That would be the last time I would see Ross in person, until I testified against him a few years later, in the case against him in Lorain County Court Of Common Pleas.

He did not leave any of the information or documentation related to the Microsoft and Compaq cases that he was handling for Erie Shores. It was extremely difficult to concentrate that entire evening. Without mentioning to anyone what had happened, I sprayed my office and kept the door closed for the remainder of the afternoon. Upon arriving home, I went to bed without dinner and arose early after very little sleep and returned to the office.

CHAPTER FIFTY TWO

I sat in my office that Thursday morning attempting to comprehend the extent of damage Ross had done to Erie Shores. A couple of hours later, around 7:00 a.m., the phone rang. On the line
was the partner in the Akron, Ohio, law firm that was representing Compaq Computer Corporation. From the tone of his voice
I could tell that he was very frustrated. He said, "Jones, what in
the hell are you trying to do, force us to proceed with this lawsuit
against your firm?" I was shocked, to put it mildly, so I attempted
to keep my composure. I knew Erie Shores was at the mercy of
both Compaq and Microsoft for what appeared to be the unethical sales actions of Anthony Mash, my sales manager, during a
twelve-month period.

I asked why he was so upset when my attorney had informed me
of the excellent progress the two had made concerning a settlement
with Compaq Computer. I was now aware of Ross's drug problem, but
it had not dawned on me that he had been negligent in the handling
of these two major cases against Erie Shores.

There were many seconds of silence, then the attorney responded, "What are you talking about? I have not seen or spoken with your attorney since you introduced him during our conference call three weeks ago."

This was now becoming too much even for me to handle. My heart skipped a beat, and my hands became clammy, knowing that the amount Compaq could be seeking in a settlement could be in the hundreds of thousands of dollars. After explaining to the attorney the unbelievable story of Ross's updates on the meetings that he was supposed to have had with him, the attorney could only sound out a quick sympathetic chuckle. He then informed me that he was ready to recommend to Compaq that they should proceed to trial, due to a lack of communication on the part of Erie Shores.

It was only after I had poured my heart and soul out to this attorney that he agreed to provide Erie Shores a three-week extension to give me time to obtain new counsel. I was also pretty sure by now that he had researched the finances of Erie Shores and knew about its poor financial condition.

After thanking the attorney and ending the call, I thanked God for giving me the words to say to this attorney that convinced him to provide the extension of time. During my prayer, the spirit brought to mind the question: If Ross had not made contact with the local Akron firm representing Compaq, then there was a great possibility he not been in contact with the local Cleveland law firm representing Microsoft. The Microsoft settlement could also number in the hundreds of thousands of dollars, if not handled properly.

I immediately placed the call to the Cleveland law firm handling the Microsoft case. The attorney handling the Microsoft case against Erie Shores answered the phone. He was surprised to hear from me since no one had communicated with him since the conference call three weeks prior, when I had introduced Attorney Ross as the lawyer handling the case for Erie Shores. I gave him the same true story I had given the lawyer representing Compaq less than an hour earlier.

This attorney immediately understood and actually felt a sincere sympathy for my plight. I was sure of this because of what happened over the next seven days.

This attorney alerted me that a mediation session between Microsoft and Erie Shores had been scheduled for the morning of June 5th, four days later. He alerted me that the session could not be rescheduled because a Microsoft corporate attorney was flying in from Microsoft headquarters in Washington State. Being aware of the condition in which Ross had left me, this gentlemen began to share some suggestions and provide some guidance about how I could possibly proceed in order to be ready for the mediation session between Microsoft and Erie Shores Computer.

First, he informed me that I would not need an attorney to represent me at the upcoming mediation session. I would need to answer questions and be as truthful and sincere as possible with my answers during the Tuesday session. He also explained that the mediator would be an attorney from one of the respected law firms in Cleveland.

━━◆◆━━

My attempt to reach Ross during the weekend was fruitless, so I made that twenty-five-mile trip to Cleveland solo on that Tuesday morning. As I parked my car, my cell phone rang. It was the "Young Lady" whose charges had been dropped because of her assistance in that major drug case. I was quite surprised to hear from her because she was supposed to have been in a witness protection program.

I could tell that she was crying and sounded angry and frightened at the same time. She stated, "Larry, have you seen Michael? I can't reach him, and he is not returning my calls."

I informed the Young Lady that I had not seen Ross for a period of time, and that we were no longer communicating.

I could not delay my meeting with Microsoft and explained this to her. Her final comments to me were, "They have used me and gotten what they wanted from me, including Michael, and now I'm alone, Mr. Jones, and I am afraid."

I am pretty sure I told her I would speak with her after my meeting, but I did not return her call because I had no answers for her questions.

I had left a concise message on Ross's voice mail about the mediation session and had asked him to represent me in spite of his prior actions, but there was no response, and he was a no-show at the mediation session. I had prayed that God would be with me in this mediation session, and that the Spirit would speak through me and provide the necessary answers.

The Microsoft corporate attorney was a white female in her mid-forties. The local attorney representing Microsoft, who had given me guidance, was a breaded white gentleman, appearing to be in his early forties. The mediator was a white male, in his late fifties.

Our initial session was as a group: the mediator, two Microsoft attorneys, and me. We introduced ourselves, and the mediator explained the rules and procedures we would follow during the mediation session. Then the corporate Microsoft attorney explained why Microsoft had filed legal charges against Erie Shores Computer Inc. and stated that Microsoft could be seeking as much as $950,000 from Erie Shores Computer.

When it was my time to speak, I did not attempt to deny the charges against Erie Shores because I had become aware of the unethical activities of Anthony Mash, Erie Shores Sales Manager, a few weeks prior to the charges being brought against Erie Shores. Mash had made some unethical decisions in his eagerness to make major purchases of Microsoft software to fulfill a large customer contract.

I explained that Erie Shores had been a Certified Reseller of Microsoft software for more than ten years and that I would never intentionally take any actions that would harm the strong relationship between the two firms. I felt pretty sure that all three persons present had seen my sincerity during my short presentation.

Because I did not have legal representation, when we separated for our sessions, the mediator accompanied me to my room. He had seen and had felt my sincerity and was now providing additional information about how a mediation session was conducted. This gentleman also provided some recommendations on how I should proceed to achieve the best outcome.

After his guidance, the mediator asked me how much I was willing to pay Microsoft to settle the case. I knew the financial condition of Erie Shores at that time, and the amount I suggested to him as a settlement made him laugh and ask if I was serious. As a settlement for what could be as much as $900,000, I told the mediator that Erie Shores was in a position to pay Microsoft $60,000 to settle the case.

After approximately fifteen minutes of additional discussions be-tween the mediator and me, he finally realized that $60,000 would be my firm offer to Microsoft to settle this case because that was all Erie Shores could afford to offer.

All of the participants regrouped, and I made additional com-ments, including a sincere plea to the Microsoft corporate attorney. I informed her that Erie Shores was in a financial position to pay Microsoft a total of $60,000 to settle the case. When I finished my presentation, all the Microsoft lead attorney could do was stare at me for what felt like ten to fifteen seconds. Only then did she begin to speak.

She said, "Mr. Jones, are you telling me that you want Microsoft to agree to settle a case that could demand hundreds of thousands of dollars, for sixty thousand dollars?"

I said, "Yes, ma'am, because that is all Erie Shores can afford to offer Microsoft."

There was more silence, and then she commented, "Mr. Jones, you are correct; Erie Shores has been an excellent partner with Microsoft for many years, and we appreciate this relationship. Mr. Mediator, I will need a few minutes in private with my local counsel."

Approximately fifteen minutes later both Microsoft attorneys re-joined the mediator and me. The corporate Microsoft attorney stated that she had come to a decision regarding the case.

She posed the question to me, "Mr. Jones, how do you propose to pay this sixty thousand dollars?"

I thought for a minute and stated that Erie Shores was in a position to pay $2,500 monthly until the total was paid. Again, the attorney stared at me in silence for another ten seconds.

She then stated, "Mr. Jones, I have no idea why I am doing this, but I am going to accept your settlement offer under the conditions you have requested." In my spirit I said a brief prayer and thanked her for her understanding and consideration.

The mediator then informed me that I could represent myself in these proceedings, but I could not represent Erie Shores Computer. This was when the lead Microsoft attorney asked if I had an attorney to sign the agreement for Erie Shores and I commented yes, because I was sure I could have John Keyse Walker, my attorney at Fauver, Tattersall & Gallagher, represent me.

These three attorneys, the two Microsoft attorneys and the mediator, had already assisted Erie Shores, and I was extremely grateful for what they had done. Then I realized that they were not finished with their legal guidance. Their concern now was how to have the settlement case avoid the media. All I could say in silence was, *thank you, God.*

The three of them began brainstorming and shortly arrived at the decision that the settlement of the case would not be publicized until Erie Shores had paid the sixty thousand dollars in full. They figured that by that time, the media would have lost interest in the case, thus putting Erie Shores in a position to avoid the negative headlines. These three attorneys then began discussing ways that they could complete the process prior to ending the meeting. The decision they made for me was that the local attorney representing Microsoft would create the appropriate document for my attorney to review and approve for my signature.

I have never attempted to explain to anyone other than to Attorney John Keyse Walker what happened in this mediation session. When John became aware of what I had accomplished during that mediation session, he could not believe what Microsoft had agreed to as a settlement. I knew that the God Spirit had used those three attorneys in that mediation session as my guardian angels.

Unfortunately, after all of the assistance provided by these attorneys, Erie Shores Computer would not have the opportunity to benefit from these successes because Erie Shores would be forced into Court Receivership by National City Bank less than four months later. This receivership also eliminated the legal proceedings of the Compaq Computer Corporation against Erie Shores.

CHAPTER FIFTY THREE

I knew very little about Ross personally and nothing about his family, his wife, his son, and his daughter. I knew that he was a resident of Avon Ohio. I missed the red flag that was right in front of me when I had to travel to the city of Lorain one evening at midnight to meet with Ross at his poorly kept office. Ross used the excuse of being very busy as the reason for the late-night meeting. I accepted his excuse, remembering the many fourteen- to eighteen-hour days I had spent during the first four years of building Erie Shores. That night I got the impression that Ross was actually living in his office.

I will never forget the day I arrived for an oil change at the Grease Monkey, at the Midway Mall. While sitting in the small waiting room, I decided to greet the two young ladies in the room because not speaking would have been totally impolite. After my greeting, they responded in kind. A couple of minutes later, I overheard a part of their conversation, and the name Michael Ross was muttered. I inquired if they knew Attorney Ross, and both ladies stared at me and said, "Yes, we know that no good son of a bitch.

We know his whole family—his sorry-ass daddy and him. He uses drugs and sells drugs and try to walk around in the county like he is an upstanding lawyer, but we know better." These two strangers had just provided me some critical information that my civic and business associates had not shared with me regarding Michael Ross, the lawyer whom I had representing my firm. Ross would later be disbarred because of his numerous improper actions as a lawyer.

It became very clear that if what these ladies were saying was true or even half or a fourth true, then the Michael Ross that had been presented to me wasn't the real Michael Ross. Now I am really concerned about this relationship for a number of reasons, but one reason haunted me more than any other: the relationship that had been created involving the construction of the Lorain County Justice Center.

I had become aware who Michael Ross really was: an individual as evil and dark as Arthur Boyd and Merceda Perry. Richard Buie and Marty Conn had covered their tracks so well that it would be a few years later before I would realize their evils.

After I successfully negotiated the financial agreement with Microsoft, I knew I would probably not see Ross again. He had received what he wanted from the "Young Lady" (sex and money) and from me (the $600,000 needed to pay his debt). He then dumped both of us, or so it appeared. I should have known that if Ross could find a way to continue to use me, he would.

⊷ ⊷

It is now around March 2003. Erie Shores was on its last leg, but I continued to be focused on keeping the firm afloat.

Since mid-2002, I had been operating both Erie Shores and New World Beverages, LLC. I knew that the chances for investments would be much better for New World Beverages than for Erie Shores.

Richard Buie and Marty Conn had not been successful in bringing in investors, so I had decided to deplete our family savings of approximately $850,000 and loans from my sister, totaling approximately $1.7 million to maintain both firms until the promised investments could arrive, including the pending $37 million off-shore loan to New World Beverages LLC. I knew there were risks, but I also knew that if I failed, my sister would be in a position to write off her and her husband's investments.

Because of their lack of financial assistance, I had decided to inform Buie and Conn that their services would no longer be needed, but just as I had decided to inform them of my decision, Buie informed me that he had been able to secure a meeting with the vice president of marketing at the Kroger Foods headquarters in Cincinnati, Ohio.

Buie and I traveled to Cincinnati and met with the Kroger vice president of marketing. Buie presented New World Beverages line of beverages, using the prepared slide presentation. He also presented chilled samples of New World's Dot Com line of beverages. I have great confidence in my ability to sell, but the power sales presentation I experienced during that session was truly out of this world. It was as though Buie had mesmerized Kroger Food's vice president of marketing. He was hanging on every word Buie spoke.

When the forty-minute session ended, this vice president had agreed to have the two of us travel to the Kroger Foods' Southwest region office in Houston, Texas, to meet with the vice president of marketing for that region.

I knew that I had seen something very rare and a little scary during the first Kroger meeting—something very powerful. I had just witnessed a level of persuasion that I had never seen before in a sales meeting. Buie was well aware that he possessed this power, and I would see him use this power again in our meeting at the Kroger Food, Houston Regional office. We exited that meeting with a $30 to $40 million open-end contract to retail our beverages in the Kroger Food stores, nationwide. This contract would also open the door for the four co-packers owned by Kroger to produce the Dot Com line of beverages. The Kroger Payton Distribution firm would agree to distribute the New World beverages.

Contents of the New World Beverages contract with Kroger Food chain included:

a. Kroger agrees to sell the Dot Com line of beverages.
b. Kroger will co pack the Dot Com line of beverages at its co packing facilities.
c. Kroger will use its Payton Distribution operations to warehouse and distribute Dot Com.
d. Kroger will entertain the possibility of branding Dot Com in an ice cream line.

I was now pretty sure that Erie Shores" and New World Beverages' financial problems were over. A conservative gross sales projection for the first two years was $22 to $27 million.

⊷⊶

What I did not understand at the time was that Richard Buie did not look at this major contract as something of value. His pleasure came from knowing that he could persuade and, when necessary, overwhelm whomever he pleased in the sales game, including when up against the most experienced corporate executives. With this Kroger success under his belt, he focused his sights on other big game.

Three weeks after the Kroger successes, Buie came up with a financing plan. New World would seek off-shore funding, and he agreed to investigate the process and locate a financial firm. I was so sure we were finally on our way to creating wealth for those involved that I posed few in-depth questions of Buie. Little did I know that Buie, the sociopath with a photographic memory, had viewed all of the successes with Kroger not as great successes for New World Beverages but as a great personal achievement. This meant that he was not at all interested in the successes of the company. After all, he was living very well from all of the scammed funds from Erie Shores. He had nothing to lose; he had invested no funds, so he could play all of his mind games without any negative business or personal consequences.

New World Beverages now had a beverage contract with Kroger Foods, a contract that would assure New World Beverages financial security. This was why I invited my sister, Brenda, and her husband to invest in New World; the success of this venture was pretty much assured. My sister and her husband invested more than $1.6 million in New World Beverages.

CHAPTER FIFTY FOUR

I have always been confident in my business acumen, especially in the areas of logistics and problem solving. Because of the teachings of my parents, my various instructors, and all of the white businessmen whom I had partnered with or had an association with there had been very few times when I even had to wonder if I had been cheated or deceived in a business deal.

Believing that people were inherently good provided a false sense of security that led me to trust persons whom I should not have trusted. Trusting people did not become a negative until I had lived for fifty years. My business associations had not put me in official contact with other African American businessmen. After being in business for fifteen years, I would begin my interactions with African Americans: business associate, Richard Buie, Dr. Arthur Boyd Jr., Dr. Merceda Perry, and Attorney Michael Ross. I had partnered with white businessmen for fifteen years, sometimes with just a handshake. After partnering with African American businessmen and professionals for less than four years, my companies and family finances were destroyed, and criminal charges were being filed against me. What's that about?

Not until I began to affiliate, associate, and partner with this African American businessman, two African American medical doctors, and an African American attorney and CPA did I experience jealousy, envy, and even hatred in my business dealings, and these were people whom I had agreed to assist financially and regarding management.

Each of these African American "professionals" had the mindset that in a business venture, for them to win, the other person would have to lose. Therefore, because of this flawed belief and the jealously and "crabs in the barrel" mentality, these "professionals" worked extremely hard to destroy joint business opportunities. They could not comprehend and understand that my firm was the "chicken that was laying the golden eggs" on which they were surviving and soon to thrive. This was why I believed that the statement "no good deed will go unpunished" was factual, especially if the statement was in the context of African American businessmen partnering in business.

In my life experiences and in my various business associations and relationships with African Americans and Caucasians, the relationships with white and Oriental businessmen have been productive, but every one of my business relationships with African American businessmen have all been unproductive and destructive.

It pains me to say this, but my family and I had better business relationships with those members of the Ku Klux Klan back in Durham, North Carolina, and their supporters than any of my business relationships established with other African American businessmen.

My twenty-five years in business confirmed that these same African American businessmen who would cheat and scam their African American business partners, when partnering with a white businessmen, would not scam or cheat their white business partners. This was why I felt that the Willie Lynch story was so profound. It appeared that most African Americans, including businessmen, interact with each other from the "crabs in the barrel" mentality.

☛☚

Erie Shores had been awarded the $4 million line of credit by National City Bank, but after the 9/11 national disaster, the $4 million line became an "asset-based" line of credit. An asset-based line of credit was an extremely restricted line of credit. In order to use this line, Erie Shores had to make a sale. Once a sale was made, Erie Shores would be able to use only 20 percent of that total sale to pay its bills.

The normal process when a bank awarded an asset-based loan or line of credit was that it also provided that firm a "working capital loan." Erie Shores Computer was not provided a working capital loan by National City Bank, even after making three working capital requests of Howard Walters, the loan officer and branch manager.

I was well aware that I was violating the terms of this loan with National City Bank, but it was critical that I kept the only mainstream African-American-owned-and-operated firm in the history of Lorain County operating.

When I made the decision to misuse the asset-based line of credit to keep Erie Shores operating, I knew at the time that Erie Shores had enough sales on the book to cover the increases in customer invoices. This is why I called the Erie Shores office staff together and informed all three of them that if anything negative arose from my decision, I would accept full responsibility.

As powerful as my logistics and ability to problem solve were, I did not see the devastation that the future held. At the time, I had reasons to be confident:

A. I was positive that the orders Erie Shores Computer had on the books would cover the funds needed for the invoice increases.

But sixty-five days after I signed the $4 million Erie Shores loan agreement with National City Bank on July 6, 2001, the United States of America was attacked on its soil for only the second time in history.

The national economies shut down for months. More than 60 percent of Erie Shores Computer sales were to federal, state, and local governmental agencies and educational agencies. Erie Shores lost more than 50 percent of those orders through cancellations. In addition, National City Bank had stipulated that its line of credit would not fund any of these governmental and educational sales.

B. Richard Buie and Marty Conn had investors lined up to invest in Erie Shores and New World Beverages LLC. Of course, it would later become clear that there were never any investors in the first place.

C. Michael Ross had promised to have investors lined up to invest in New World Beverages. Again, there were no investors.

D. My sister and her husband invested more than $1 million in New World Beverages, with the understanding that additional investments were forthcoming.

Eventually, I would face the harsh reality that only my sister's funds and our personal family funds would be invested. All of the planning, logistics, and investing could not stop or even delay the tragedy that was beginning to be revealed.

In early June of 2003, National City Bank filed charges against Erie Shores Computer Inc., and a court receiver took control of Erie Shores.

After this filing, I focused my attention on the success of New World Beverages. A few months later, New World Beverages was awarded the Kroger Food Chain contracts. I knew if these contracts were handled correctly, we would all be successful, and I would be able to repay the funds to National City Bank and pull Erie Shores from the jaws of bankruptcy and court receivership.

I wasn't through learning my lessons, but I had learned enough to know that if you are working with sociopaths, no matter how successful you think you are, the projects will always end in failure. This was exactly what happened to the New World Beverages contracts that would be awarded by the Kroger Food Chain. Buie's grand scheme required a massive sum of money to achieve, and I went along with this plan, a plan Buie and Conn knew would fail. Failure did not matter to them because they had already scammed over a million dollars. The off-shore funds that were supposed to be provided to New World Beverages did not materialize. I would never know if these funds were real, even after the trip to Costa Rica, because once the group that we were negotiating with to provide the funds realized that I was being investigated by the FBI, not only was the possible $37 million fund opportunity cancelled, the $112,000 that had been paid for the fund services was also lost.

CHAPTER FIFTY FIVE

After the 9/11/2001 national disaster and the great loss of Erie Shores' customer orders, and after realizing that there would be no investments by Richard Buie and Marty Conn's contacts, I was forced to face the harsh reality that lay in front of me. I felt the best way to confront the problem was to send a detailed letter to Mr. William MacDonald, the vice chairman and president of National City Bank, explaining the actions I had taken and to provide factual information as to how Erie Shores would be able to correct this fund shortfall within a twelve-month period. This repayment of funds was based on the fact that Erie Shores had been awarded its Government Services Administration, (GSA) schedule.

I was pretty sure that I would at least receive a response from Mr. MacDonald, but no response came. Instead Mr. MacDonald started immediate legal action against Erie Shores and approximately three months after my letter, Erie Shores Computer was forced into court receivership.

Approximately four months after Erie Shores was forced into receivership (12/03/2003), I sent a sworn affidavit and a copy of the
letter that I had sent to Mr. MacDonald at National City Bank to US
Attorney Gregory White.

This sworn affidavit included vital and factual information about
who had committed the fraud in the FirstMerit Bank $2 million loans
and how it was done and how this scam had cost Erie Shores great
financial losses. I also shared the Star Beverage connection to money
being funneled to terrorists in the Middle East.

I never received a response form US Attorney White nor any of his
assistant attorneys. Instead it appeared that US Attorney White had
the FBI focus its investigation solely on me for the next approximately
thirty-four months. While serving as Lorain County Prosecutor, Mr.
White had been involved in the investigation of the FirstMerit Bank
March 2000 loan fraud beginning in mid-2001, and he continued
his investigation after becoming the US Attorney for the Northern
District of Ohio in early 2003.

Instead of focusing the investigation on all persons and entities
involved in the March 2000 loan signing and activities, US Attorney
White, after assuming that position in early 2003, directed all of the
agency's attention on the indicting and prosecuting of me. It continued to be difficult for me to believe that Gregory White would hold
such a viscous grudge against me for my 1987 legal actions against
Lorain County.

Realizing that Richard Buie had agreed to testify against me for
the US Attorney (speculation from facts), I thought: What had Buie
told US Attorney White that would convince him to trust him? Then
it came to me why Greg White could have additional reasons to want
me prosecuted.

Eric Nord, Scribner Fauver, and Mal Mixon were the most powerful Republicans in Lorain County and Northern Ohio. Therefore, when Gregory White decided to run for a US Congressional seat against Sherrod Brown, these three men headed the support for White in his campaign. Sherrod Brown, the Democratic incumbent, defeated Greg White and retained his congressional seat. A couple of weeks after Greg White's defeat, I met with Scrib for some legal advice. During our meeting we discussed the congressional campaign and the fact that Sherrod Brown had defeated White.

Scrib knew that I had voted for Sherrod and had suggested that I should not run for any elected office in Lorain County while my company was based in the county. I was the closest friend of color that Attorney Fauver had ever had, so he shared, in confidence, a number of secrets. One of those secrets shared was that he was relieved when Sherrod Brown defeated Greg White. He stated that he did not feel that Greg had the temperament to be an effective congressman because it appeared that it was impossible for him to control that temper of his. I had shared this information with only one other person: Richard Buie.

I know for a fact that volumes of incriminating evidence had been uncovered against Boyd and Perry by the FBI in the March 2000 $2 million loan scam at FirstMerit Bank, but all of this evidence were ignored and not used by the US Attorney's office, even after the Lorain County Court of Common Pleas had awarded Erie Shores and me a $1,423,352.64 judgment against Boyd, Perry, and Star Beverage.

As I mentioned to you earlier, the Federal Bureau of Investigation began its investigation of FirstMerit Bank, Erie Shores Computer, and me in early 2002, after Dr. Boyd Jr. and Dr. Perry submitted false complaints to the Elyria city police and the FBI.

This investigation and court proceeding of fraud, related to this March 2000 $2 million loan to Star Beverage Inc. by FirstMerit Bank, continued for more than four years, without the case ever going to trial.

In November 2005, Special FBI Agent, David Lyons and a Lorain County detective arrived at my home and began inquiring about the Erie Shores' National City Bank loan. I was now positive that the US Attorney, the FBI, and the state investigators had finally read my December 2003 sworn affidavit and had investigated and now understood the connection between the March 2000 FirstMerit Bank loan scam and how this had led to my National City Bank loan problems. After all, US Attorney Gregory White had received my sworn affidavit almost twenty-four months prior. Instead, Special Agent David Lyons presented a letter that informed me that I was being investigated by the FBI and the US Attorney's office. Records will show that I, along with Erie Shores Computer, Bruce Stevens, and FirstMerit Bank, had been under investigation since early 2001 by the same FBI agent, Special Agent, David Lyons. Special Agent Lyons is the person who knew the in-depth details concerning the FirstMerit loan scam and the activities of those involved.

I can only wonder if Agent Lyons's conscious was clear after his non-action in this case, especially after I had provided him loads of documents and information, including a copy of the fraudulent $69 million navy contract. I have no doubt in my mind that FBI Special Agent David Lyons had enough information and evidence against Dr. Arthur Boyd Jr. and Dr. Merceda Perry to have the US Attorney file charges against them in mid-2002, prior to Perry's massive heart attack. I am also well aware that Agent Lyons had to follow the orders and wishes of his boss and the directives of the US Attorney for the Northern District of Ohio.

Special Agent Lyons would refuse to mention or discuss anything related to the FirstMerit Bank scam; the scam he had investigated for four years. His total focus was my activities related to the Erie Shores Computer $4 million line of credit at National City Bank. US Attorney Gregory White had known since December 3, 2003 about my actions regarding the Erie Shores line of credit at National City Bank because of the sworn affidavit I FedExed to him on that date. From this meeting, I had a real positive feeling that something very bad was about to happen. I would soon learn how the wheels of justice turn when the master wheel turner is a long-time law enforcer and adversary.

No official charges were ever filed in the FirstMerit Bank fraud, but unofficial charges were brought against me by the US Attorney, which enhanced its case against me in the National City Bank charges.

CHAPTER FIFTY SIX

In April 2006, I was indicted on approximately sixty federal criminal charges and approximately fifteen state criminal charges. The state charges were related to my alleged activities with Michael Ross while he served as the first African American Lorain County commissioner. It became very clear why I was the only one now being investigated. Fear gripped me for a few minutes after remembering the threat in 1987 that then, Lorain County prosecutor, Gregory White, had made against me in my attorney's office in downtown Cleveland, Ohio. That threat, "I am going to get you" was made after Lorain County prosecutor, Gregory White, had to sign documents that awarded a $115,000 to Erie Shores Computer Inc. Damn, after all of these years avoiding Gregory White, I had now put myself in a position , where US Attorney Gregory White could fulfill the threat he had made.

Not one single charge was ever filed against Dr. Arthur Boyd Jr., Bruce Stevens, or any of the FirstMerit executives. Dr. Perry had died in June of 2002.

By this time, I was now astute enough to realize the following:

A. A defense against the US Attorney is a losing battle. The facts about whether I was innocent or guilty were no longer of importance.

B. A defense against the US Attorney in federal court would be extremely expensive. My attorney had already charged me more than $60,000, and we were not even close to a trial date. Once my attorney realized that I had no more funds, including no funds off shore, and that US Attorney Gregory White had a personal vendetta against me, he began to suggest that I agree to a plea.

C. I contend that my attorney and the Assistant US Attorney "officially" handling my case were good friends and members of the same synagogue.

I contend that if I had been aware of the relationship between my attorney, Larry Zukerman, and US Assistant Attorney, John Siegel, and how both wanted to please the US Attorney, I would have enlisted a different law firm to represent me in this criminal case. Too late would I learn that because of these established relationships, I would be defending myself against the US Attorney's Office, the US District Court, and the attorney whom I had already paid $60,000 for my defense. Too late would I realize that I really had no one defending me.

D. US Attorney Gregory White had been and would continue to be personally involved in my case and had made the decision that the charges against me would continue in both the federal and state courts. Former Lorain County detective Dennis Will was now the Lorain County prosecutor, so I knew my chances in state court would be the same as in federal court.

This continuation of charges in state court was mainly for the purpose of successfully indicting and convicting Michael Ross, the person who, as Lorain County prosecutor, Gregory White had been attempting to indict for a number of years. He now saw a great opportunity to use me and my situation to accomplish what he had been unable to accomplish for approximately ten years; to indict and convict Michael Ross.

My initial decision was to fight this selective prosecution against me by the FBI and the US Attorney, but the following are facts and actions that finally convinced me to change my mind and accept a plea in the US District Court:

1. I remember the threat that then Lorain County prosecutor, Gregory White, had made against me in 1987.

2. After sending US Attorney White the sworn affidavit and a copy of the letter to Mr. William MacDonald, vice chairman of National City Bank, on 12/03/2003, I received no response.

3. I knew that then Detective Dennis Will (a mentee of Prosecutor Gregory White) had investigated Michael Ross in a case in Columbus Ohio and was informed that Ross was attempting to use a fraudulent power of attorney in my name to purchase three parcels of land. Detective Will had informed the mortgage broker, Mr. Gregory Filbrun, that he would contact me about this attempted fraud as soon as he returned to Lorain County. Detective Will never contacted me about this attempted fraud against me by Michael Ross.

4. Dennis Will, now Lorain County prosecutor and US Attorney Gregory White's mentee, filed the state criminal charges, based on the federal charges against me, at the directions of US Attorney Gregory White.

5. After my legal counsel attended a meeting where US Attorney Gregory White and approximately six of his assistant US Attorney's were present and US Attorney Gregory White made the comment, "Nothing moves in Lorain County unless Jones knows about it," my attorney also informed me that US Attorney White thought that I was involved in the activities that the FBI was investigating related to city of Cleveland, Mayor Michael White, and his friend Nate Gray.

My attorney realized that Gregory White appeared to have something personal against me. After updating me on the meeting, I explained to him why US Attorney White did not like me and about the threat he had made against me in 1987, while serving as Lorain County prosecutor.

6. After my attorney warned me about the powers that Greg White possessed as US Attorney, it appeared that he was willing to destroy the lives of members of my family (my daughter, my sister, and my wife) and anyone else to get me convicted.

After much prayer and two meetings with my family, it became very clear to me that I had no other logical choice but to agree to a plea. This plea would protect my family but send me to federal prison for thirty-seven months and force me to testify against Michael Ross on the state charges that had been filed against the two of us. If I refused to testify, the state charges against me would not become a part of my plea agreement. I agreed to the plea and at Ross's trial in 2009, testified against him. My testifying against Ross would include confirming charges against him for crimes that I knew and the county prosecutor knew Ross had not committed.

CHAPTER FIFTY SEVEN

In July of 2006, I stood before Judge Gwin in his Cleveland, Ohio, US District Courtroom and accepted the plea that had been drawn up by US Attorney Gregory White. This was my first visit to a US District Courtroom. As soon as I entered the room, I felt great intimidation: the quietness, the richness of the floors and walls and the ceiling of dark wood. The most intimidating of all was the elevation of the judge's seat above where I was standing. I suggest to you that the judge was seated, at minimum, seven feet above the level where everyone else was standing. It was like speaking before deity.

At the time I accepted my plea in Judge Gwinn's federal courtroom, I received some consolation when the judge commented, "Mr. Jones, it appears that you did not use any of the funds misappropriated in this case for personal use." The judge proceeded to explain why he could not reduce my sentence more than he had already. All of this occurred a few minutes before I would come in contact with US Attorney Gregory White in the rear of the courtroom.

Judge Gwinn asked me if I was accepting this plea of my own free will, and I stated, yes; knowing all the time that I was accepting this plea to protect my family and under extreme duress. I remember saying to myself; 'So mote it be", because I knew I had no other logical choice. What father, husband, or brother would not accept a plea under these circumstances?

As I was departing the courtroom, US Attorney Gregory White was standing by the exit door. As I approached him, I had no idea what my actions would be when I came close to him. I am quite sure I had said a brief prayer, and upon my approach, I extended my hand and shook his. As he took my hand, US Attorney White, that same person who had threatened me nineteen years earlier, looked into my eyes and then dropped his head and said, "Man, I'm sorry."

I had put myself in a position where US Attorney Gregory White had offered me a lose-lose proposition: accept a plea that would send me to federal prison for thirty-seven months or expose my family members to federal legal proceedings; and now he was telling me that he was sorry! I did not respond to his apology. I just proceeded to exit the courtroom.

After this plea, I was now attempting to comprehend what had happened to me during the past six years. I had gone from being a successful businessman, civic leader, director of a bank, trustee of a hospital, and a staunch believer in the fairness of the US justice system to experiencing firsthand the reality that legal power in the wrong hands can perform evil in the guise of justice. If I had deserved to have all of the charges that had been filed against me, I would have accepted what happened to me and the resulting extreme treatment, without comment.

In May 2003, prior to National City Bank filing for receivership of Erie Shores Computer, the Erie Shores' loan account was assigned to the Distressed Loan division of National City. The Erie Shores distressed account loan officer was Michael McNiery. After Mr. McNiery became familiar with the Erie Shores account and after two meetings with me, he began to share suggestions about how I could possibly resolve the Erie Shores financial situation. Because of the 9-11 national disaster, he had seen this problem numerous time during the past twenty-four months. Over a period of four weeks, Mr. McNiery made the following suggestions: (1) find a way to cover the losses—that did not materialize; (2) send a letter to the bank's chairman, providing evidence that Erie Shores had the upcoming contracts under the GSA Schedule, to cover the bank losses. McNiery suggested that I send this letter because he had worked with three other firms since the 9/11 disaster that had similar financial problems, and the bank had worked with these firms in-house, and they had been given time to resolve their issues. Following Mr. McNiery's advice, after learning of my relationship with Mr. MacDonald, McNiery suggested that I submit a letter to Mr. MacDonald. Mr. MacDonald was chairman of National City Bank, and I was a member of the President's Council of Minority Business owners, of which Mr. MacDonald was a member of the corporate board and a mentor and supporter of the twenty-member President's Council.

Instead of receiving a response for Mr. MacDonald, my account was removed from Mr. McNiery, and the receivership proceedings were initiated. Less than two weeks later, I would learn that Mr. McNiery had been transferred to a Toledo, Ohio, branch of the bank.

Mr. McNiery had confirmed that three white business owners with similar financial problems had been treated totally different from how Erie Shores and I were being treated after the 9-11 tragedy.

But I really could not use this difference in treatment as an excuse because I was well aware, as an African American businessman, that I could not expect any favors from banks, even FirstMerit Bank, the bank where I had served as a director for seven years.

Because of my belief that if wrong was brought upon me, that wrong would be transformed in to something good, as strange as it may sound, after I accepted the plea agreement under extreme duress, I felt like a thousand-pound weight had been lifted from my shoulders. Even though I did not accept the apology of US Attorney Gregory White, that apology confirmed that he had become aware that he had taken his vendetta against me to extremes that would destroy my future.

These trials and tribulations had been very hard on me, but what was more important to me was the extreme fear and stress these legal procedures had caused my family, especially my wife, Barbara. The US Attorney's office had tried and convicted me in the media long before I was fully aware of what was happening to me. The FBI had visited many of the African American and Hispanic leaders in Lorain County prior to my arrest, not to gain information about me but to put the fear of God in each of them so that they would be very hesitant to assist me in any way. US Attorney White had remembered the major support I had garnered from the African American and Hispanic communities when I was awarded $115,000 by the commissioners in 1987. This time he had nullified any community support, so when I sent approximately fifty letters out to the community requesting financial assistance for my defense, only four persons responded. Later I would be informed that those from whom I had requested support admitted that they were hesitant to assist me in any way.

I did not totally fault the actions of US Attorney Gregory White because I knew I had put myself in a position where he could file charges against me. My financial destruction and destroyed reputation had been caused by the evil, cunning, and deceptive lies and actions of an African American business associate, two African American medical doctors, and an African American attorney. The lies and actions of these individuals led me to take illegal actions to keep Erie Shores operating during the 9/11 attack on the United States of America. The lies and deceit put me in a position to make financial decisions that delivered me into the hands of US Attorney Gregory White. Gregory White had been put in a position where he could fulfill his 1987 threat against me.

CHAPTER FIFTY EIGHT

I will always remember that early morning in 2006 when a divine advance warning came to Barbara and me. This warning alerted us to dangers coming our way. It was early February 2006, after driving my daughter Galan and a couple of her friends to school. Galan was a freshman at Elyria High. Upon returning home, as I entered the house form the garage, my eyes were forced to the open Bible laying on the kitchen counter. It was as if an extremely bright light was shining directly on the open Bible. There was no logical reason why the light appeared to be brighter on the area of the counter where the Bible lay. As I approached the Bible, I could see that it was opened to the third chapter of Proverbs. As I viewed closer, my attention was immediately drawn to verses 21 through 26. Those verses read:

> My son, preserve sound judgment and discernment,
> do not let them out of your sight: they will be life for
> you, an ornament to grace your neck. Then you will go
> on your way in safety, and your foot will not stumble;
> when you lie down, you will not be afraid; when you lie

down, your sleep will be sweet. Have no fear of sudden disaster or the ruin that the wicked plan, for the Lord will be your confidence and will keep your foot from being snared.

I immediately knew that there was a message for my family and me in these passages of Proverbs.

Barbara was upstairs at the time, and I called to her to join me downstairs at the kitchen counter. After I explained to her what had happened to me since I had entered the house, she looked at me and said, "Larry, maybe this passage of Proverbs is a warning for us about what is coming, and that we should prepare ourselves."

My daughter Tara and her family lived in Columbus, Ohio, and attended the church where my old friend, Reverend Dr. William S. Wheatley was pastor. To keep abreast of his teachings and preaching, Tara always sent Barbara and me a tape of his sermons.

That same afternoon after the "Bible on the counter" incident, I decided to listen to the tape of Rev. Wheatley's sermon that he had given the prior Sunday. His sermon was taken from Proverbs 3:23–26! What a confirmation!

When Barbara returned from work that afternoon, I informed her that the sermon Wheatley had preached the prior Sunday was taken from the twenty-third through the twenty-sixth verses of Proverbs chapter three. We were now sure that we were being warned of the coming dangers. We also knew that we were being told not to worry about this danger because the God Spirit would be with us.

CHAPTER FIFTY NINE

Less than four weeks later, I was indicted on more than sixty federal criminal counts and more than fifteen state criminal counts. Approximately six weeks prior, I obtained Larry Zukerman as my legal counsel. He had communicated with US Attorney Gregory White, and an agreement had been reached that if or when charges were filed against me, I would turn myself in to the authorities—or so we thought.

On this special day in April 2006, I was home for a while in the morning hours but later had a meeting on the west side of Cleveland. When that meeting was completed, I had planned to return home for the day, but a divine spirit compelled me to go to Independence, Ohio, and have an unscheduled meeting with the manager of the Holiday Inn to discuss and schedule an upcoming New World Beverage function. This meeting with the Holiday Inn manager had already been planned for the next day because I already had a 9:00 a.m. meeting scheduled in Independence with an Insurance firm. Now, for some unknown reason, I had decided to drive thirty-five miles, to Independence, knowing that I would be required to return that next day.

While I was in my meeting at the Holiday Inn, Barbara called on my cell. When I answered, she whispered, "Larry, they are here to get you!" There were more than nine US marshals, deputy sheriffs, highway patrol, and Elyria police cars surrounding the cul-de-sac on which we lived. I would later find out that the same number of law enforcement authorities had surrounded my office building at the Elyria Midway Mall.

All of this show of force occurred after US Attorney Gregory White had promised my attorney that I would be allowed to turn myself in to the authorities. US Attorney Gregory White had lied to my attorney, and I knew why. I also knew that the God Spirit was again guiding me and confirming a divine presence by having led me away from home that afternoon.

US Attorney Gregory White had decided to make my arrest a public spectacle so that all the media in Northern Ohio could view it. He wanted the public to see pictures and videos of me in handcuffs, being lead from my residence. All I can tell you is that the God Spirit confounded the plans of US Attorney Gregory White that day, and he was denied his planned public embarrassment of my family and me.

After my conversation with Barbara, I proceeded immediately to travel the approximately six miles to Attorney Zukerman's office in downtown Cleveland. After explaining what was happening at my home, he did not appear to be surprised. He immediately placed a call to the US Attorney's office and arranged for me to turn myself in to the Lorain County sheriff's office that afternoon. Upon our (my attorney's and my) arrival at the county jail, as I exited from the vehicle, a US marshal approached me to handcuff me. We were less than twenty-five yards from the entrance into the jail. Before the marshal could handcuff me, my attorney questioned why I had to be cuffed to walk such a short distance. I was now under the authority of the Lorain County sheriff's office, and the Lorain County Deputy on duty confirmed that he did not feel that I needed to be cuffed to walk such a short distance. This was a great blessing because Barbara had arrived at the jail and was viewing all of this action from her vehicle.

I was booked and spent my first night in incarceration. I was in a holding cell along with approximately fifteen other inmates. The next morning the *Chronicle Telegram* was delivered to one of the fifteen inmates, and my photo and a half-page article was on the front page of the local section. For the next two hours I was treated like a celebrity by these inmates. I was depressed because I was incarcerated, but I felt a sadness for those inmates who viewed the article the US Attorney's office had provided the *Chronicle*. These inmates were proud to associate with me during those two hours prior to the agents picking me up and delivering me to the federal holding facility in downtown Cleveland.

I remember well, the conversation that took place with the agent who shared the back seat of the vehicle with me during the trip to downtown Cleveland. This young man was very courteous and made sure that I was as comfortable as possible while riding with my hands cuffed behind my back. The highlights of this young agent's comments were: "Jones, I'm not sure why the attorney's office held off so long in their decision to arrest you". Where were you when we came to arrest you? Had someone alerted you that we were coming? I was in that first session when we interviewed you in the presence of your attorney, We knew then that this Richard Buie and that Conn guy were your biggest problems because of the major amount of funds they received from your firm." End of comments by the federal agent.

CHAPTER SIXTY

J ust knowing that I had been warned, more importantly, the way we
had been warned about the coming nightmare, gave us the courage
to begin a long and dark eight-year journey. I was now hurt, wounded,
and filled with hate—hate that turned to wanting vengeance, vengeance against the scamming medical doctor. I couldn't take any action against his partner because he was already dead. I didn't need
to take any action against the attorney because the feds and Ohio authorities were after him. At this time I was beginning to realize that the
portal to my problems had begun with Richard Buie. He had brought
the doctors and the Italian Jewish scam artist into my business and my
personal life. The only evil and dark person Buie had not introduced
me to was the attorney. I met him because I felt the need to assist an
African American politician make history in Lorain County, Ohio.

I began to plan how to do great harm to the doctor. I had no idea
how to do it, but I wanted to remove him from the land of the living.
Shortly after my seventy-plus indictments, my plea agreement and all

the media coverage, out of nowhere, a special visitor, whom I had not seen in years, arrived in Elyria and requested a private meeting. Upon arriving at the restaurant, I ordered a Grand Marnier, and he ordered coconut shrimp. He never drank because he was concerned that alcohol would affect his nervous system.

His first comment was, "Mr. Jones, I owe you my life, and I am here to assist you in any way I can. We sat at the bar, and as he began to speak, his voice lowered, and his stare became cold and dark, as though he were looking through me. At this point, there was no doubt why my old friend had come to Elyria. I knew this was the vehicle that had been sent from the dark side to fulfill my wishes. The last time I was aware of him using his special skills was while seeing action during the brief Desert Storm conflict.

After our brief meeting, I drove him over to Harvard Avenue on the east side of Cleveland. Upon our return to the restaurant, I was provided a phone and a number to dial if I wanted this individual eliminated. All I needed to do was use that special phone and dial that special number prior to the special date. Let's just say, the doctor will never know how close he came to being exterminated.

I had come to realize that I would receive no help from the legal system because the person at the head of the US Attorney's Office was too busy fulfilling his vendetta against me. Therefore, this was my opportunity to become the enforcer and make the doctor pay for the role that he had played in destroying my life.

Our meeting ended, and we shook hands, and the special visitor disappeared into the dark. I never even saw his mode of transportation. "Was this for real?" was the question that took control of my mind. I knew that it was real because of the special phone I held in my hand. A phone that, if dialed, would end the life of one of my enemies.

This meeting took place approximately five minutes from my home, and by the time I returned home that evening, I was more than sure that I would never use that special phone to call that special number. I knew that a divine spirit had shown me that what I thought I wanted to do was something I could never do or agree to have done. From the dark side and out of nowhere, this special visitor had come to make me an offer that I was now sure I had to refuse. Oh, but what a feeling of supreme power this visitor from the dark side had given me, just when it appeared that all power had been taken from me. I was pretty sure that he continued to stay abreast of the news in Lorain County and Northeast Ohio, from wherever he might have been.

I thought that I wanted to eliminate this individual because of what he and his partners had done to my family, my company, and me. For a few months, I had gone to bed with a headache and had awakened the next morning with a more extreme headache and a stomachache. At that time, I was sure that the only action that would provide me relief was to get the vengeance that I was seeking. But the God Spirit knew what was in my heart and proceeded to provide me the opportunity to get the vengeance that I thought I was seeking.

I began to pray that this hatred would be removed from my heart and mind, not really thinking that I would immediately feel a change. But not more than two weeks had passed when I awakened one morning and experienced a feeling of peace and tranquility like I had never experienced before. After that morning, the hatred I had for these individuals began to ease, and after a few months, this hatred had subsided, and as time passed, I was able to forgive these individuals for destroying everything that Barbara and I had built over a twenty five-year period. I cannot explain it, nor do I understand, but what I am sure of is that the guidance and revelations that were taking place in my life were far beyond my mental powers and abilities to understand and to achieve on my own.

CHAPTER SIXTY ONE

Some of the comfort that I felt was because of the content of the plea to which I had agreed. The US Attorney's office and FBI would no longer officially harass my daughter, Tara, my sister, Brenda, or my wife, Barbara.

I now must prepare Barbara, Tara, Galan, Bennett, and myself for the next seventeen months of waiting to begin my thirty-seven months of incarceration. My mind has been full of thoughts: What does Barbara think of me? Will she wait for me? What do my children (Tara, Galan, and Bennett) think of me? Why did God permit this to happen to me? And now that this hate has been removed from me, does this mean that God will punish those enemies of mine?

I am now quite pleased that the God Spirit has protected my wife, daughter, and sister from any future legal actions.

Only God really knew what was in store for my family and for me, but now the fear that had engulfed me for more than seven years no longer existed.

The seventeen months that I had to wait prior to serving my thirty-six-month sentence, has made it feel as though I were really serving a fifty-six-month prison sentence.

This is now the end of my past and the beginning of my future.

Note: The second book of my memoir will cover the seventeen months prior to incarceration, my thirty-seven months of incarceration, and my life after release.

An Ohio Businessman's Journey
"A Light in the Darkness"

My new life, enhanced wisdom, understanding and new thought process, manifested itself; even through the darkness.

Mr. Larry D Jones, you are hereby instructed by the Bureau of Prisons (BOP) to surrender yourself to the medium-level Federal Correctional Institution at Loretto, Pennsylvania. You are expected to arrive at 1700 hours on December 17, 2007.

But Sir, Judge Gwinn had recommended that I serve my time at the Federal Prison Camp at Morgantown, West Virginia, not behind bars and electrical and barbed-wire fences in a medium-level security prison!

.

www.ingramcontent.com/pod-product-compliance
Lightning Source LLC
Chambersburg PA
CBHW060332200326
41519CB00011BA/1912